William Blake

Paul Fearne

chipmunkapublishing
the mental health publisher

Paul Fearne

All rights reserved, no part of this publication may be reproduced by any means, electronic, mechanical photocopying, documentary, film or in any other format without prior written permission of the publisher.

>Published by
>Chipmunkapublishing
>United Kingdom

http://www.chipmunkapublishing.com

Copyright © Paul Fearne 2023

ISBN 9781783826759

This book is addressed to the 18th century English Romantic poet and artist, William Blake. This book can be seen as a companion piece to be read alongside Blake's oeuvre.

'Improvement makes strait roads; but the crooked roads without Improvement are roads of Genius'.
William Blake

I have endeavoured to follow Blake with this maxim, but have found myself editing as well. My editing style is loose, so lends itself naturally to Blake's thoughts. There is evidence that Blake edited his work as well. My lot is to edit, but leave it rough. I hope Blake approves.

Paul Fearne

William Blake

Blake – Are you the one to see things clearly? Is this what we want, to lay down our hearts, and rattle our bones? To this, I say to you – be beyond things, and more importantly, be the treasure! There can be no greater strength than this.

And here, where the fruit is without mark, the levity we seek is enough to fill our bowl to the brim. And then, despite the way we nestle, there is a groove in the Dias that does not trickle. I have heard it said, that joints in fibre never last.

Blake – And now, when the forest bleeds with berries, the noise of a thousand weary lives come in from the rain. There is here a part in the semblance of things, that has as its traipsing the sort of hush that doesn't need the respite of the unlucky!

So in belief, there is a watch cry, that tenders no time, nor resonates with the few. Do not concern yourself, the testament to the trail is here marked out. What we live with, is the temporal, and the waste of each passing breath. We will not lag – despite.

Blake – are these your runnings, that so possessed you, that out of sight, we see them fawn? In between the lark, and the touchstone, there resides more than the whole, and less than its partner. Due course, and invigoration. We will come.

Like a shape in the middle of things, mischief runs through it. But when we course, we do so for love. But what is that, in itself? It is how we are carried away on steel pinions. There is a sense we have that an armistice brings tomorrow.

Blake – do you sing, wherefore and forthwith? Is this the bend in the stone that whispers home? Can we measure the load by its embarking? I have found a way, that swamps as it tallies, that comes full circle, as moss on a lint tray. Do not evoke.

Which way do we go? Which way do we see? Have you the bounty of the tether? Is this what we say when things are grey? We have never known salt, or the bitterest of fruits. Do we sense what is in the mill grind? Much for the better – it just must.

Blake – is this the way you move? Is this the gloom that follows after? Can we say of ourselves that we are in the tomb? Do you say to yourself, this is next? I will never follow to the vision point. And this is what I say, never decreasing.

Forward, and through – around, and a-rush. There is tenacity enough to see the end sparkle. And then, without trying, a mish-mash of things to consider. Do we follow in haste, or do we edge closer to that which is withholden. We shall see.

Blake – Does the shine of it wear the robe, and do you see yourself without a reaction? In early life you went to art school. Did you find it to your liking? Did you find your way through it? It had an effect though.

And then, without recourse to the seam of it, the light of the night is found, and lo, a re-cognition of all things. I have sensed what comes next, and here, where we love what comes next, the rattle bag of hope has as its strata a fine find.

Blake – does all this point to bliss? Who would have thought difficulties would transpire? And then a ratio in the daylight. A seeking that only lends the trace, the trace of all. Come and be a mast head as a squall rears up. We will only tend.

Despite the way we walk, despite the motion of the stars – despite what comes, there is an old saying. It mesmerises as it sinks – it comes as it goes. And what does it say, but all that is. In this saying is the want of strangers. We are told.

Blake – Do the windows shake for you? Are you inclined to wander to further places? Does the rain come in symmetric ways? Has the feeling we had shown for you come in full stride? Is this what we wait for, again, again? Blake, anon.

Vociferous, and the one hand for show. A knack that has as twenty, is all that we can handle. Be the belief in store of majesty encountered. Be what is left, we have found our direction. Be the gulf between us, and what will be, will certainly be.

Blake – Is there something remis that doesn't fall? Is there something in the weave of all that is? Do we find ourselves without reclusion? There is something more to tell, but the antidote of which is a misnomer. Be the feathers on the tree, yes.

There comes a solace in the way of it. There is nothing we can help. But despite our reluctance, we court an amusing semblance. Do not be delectable in this land. There comes a trojan, that heats on mass, and deliberates through to the soles.

Blake – a smoothness, that runs as the arcs on fairest flooring. And now we wait, and see what the dawn will take as her own. Do not be belligerent in the storm. Just hold on the mast, and await your fate. There will come many things.

William Blake

Mannerisms in the citadel – coldness in the heart. We drew blood, and never guessed its time. There is a sustenance in amongst it – a sustenance that wheels away. The tightness that seems as it dives is more that we can blight. Be great.

Blake – cast a spell on me, and let it linger. My passion is like yours, that does not define itself to roughish dreams or bliss encumbered sense. Off to the land with the lot of you! There begins an adventure of a thousand wishings!

Come now, do not pout. A breeze for all that comes to pass. A sense we have that the mind is like the air, clear of intransigence's and of nature. Be the reckoning of positioning, the tale that will tell won't be cast off, that is for sure.

Blake – do be strong! Be stronger than us! We have the might of landed peers, but not what is in the fashion of the readiness of desire. The thought of this belies the notion of the today of it all. Here we come! With not just a tale of speed.

And there it is, a vastness that contains all. Be the blanket to my will, and I will be your calm, that lingers on the sounds of each arching breath. Come and see for the sake of it. Come and see, see what the dragon has maintained. Be rough – yes.

Blake – the style of it suits you, my dear. And
then, with nothing else to draw on, a sense of the
senseless, that argues back at the commonness
of it all. Have I found the way – there is no telling –
but the ease of the departure wins new appeal.

Guessing what is next, we fill our laden hearth
with gifts from the beyond. And here, where
measures are given in second hand amounts,
there is more to placate us than we thought
possible. I will run for you, so that you will never
catch up.

Blake – a misguidance that lingers, that has no
countenance, nor surmise. A thought to drown the
unwary – be here so that you may thrive. Just in
time, the resonances of a fleeting migration, come
with us as we walk. We will take what we need.

There comes a place, with each fawning breath,
that knows its measure, without the simplest kind.
And now, when we love, we do so with feeling,
and soul, and mind, and all the transportations of
deliverance. Find us, I hear you say. We will.

Blake – casting our shores to new lengths. Being
right in the middle. Having the whistle to plum.
Being sure, and enough. There rates a mighty
boon. And then, despite the catch, we feed on dry
lagoons and savoury delights.

William Blake

Hanging on, with the strength of comingled souls. Do this with tension, and the foremost thought inside will inflame, and carry you there. Despite worn out divisions in ice cold conditions, there will be more to see on the plains, again.

Blake – moisture where there was none. And more – water in store. We come to see ourselves anew, and see that part of us that we never thought possible, thrive. That is all we should say, not with dismay. Only the accomplished dance this dance.

The tempest exerts its influence deep into our lives. But what is this, the sunlight to our stars. But what is this, the entrenched and the battered. We believe again, but what of the first, the magnificent and the bold? Be exceeding, we are told.

Blake – is the thing we see right in the middle? Does it sharpen our need to digress? Are we the ones to be gathered, like sand in the pit? Come closer, let the verbs of tenacity speak to us, and never let go. We find something to show.

A ringing in the fold of June. There comes a maze, that is not for the yearning. We sense that life is ours for the keeping. Be below the mark, happenstance will reign. There is night, and there is night. Keep calm, a withholding to be sure.

Blake – There comes a nuance that has love as its bay. And here, where the trial is for forbearance, there listens carefully for the sounds of dismay. Come now, there is more to us than this. We weave, but in what colour? We sing, but when?

Hoping for the sand to be itself. Raining shards like it was winter. A motion that laughs at us. And here, a formidable opponent, one who lacks nothing but the breeze and the timbre. There can only be what is left. There can only be…

Blake – are you allowed – allowed to hop on the whispered heart and have done with the stars as they might? Do not vie for it, it is yours. It is a gift writ large on the soles of worldly feet. What have we mentioned, but the sacrosanct and the sage like.

Having the station at hand. Leaving things that little bit sanguine. There is now a way to sit, that doesn't entail the vengeance of the night. Be tired, in a tired land, and your senses will accrue a height that transposes all it encounters.

Blake – Are you so ardent in your passion, that Los cannot touch you? Is this the way we dive, in sync, and with treble the utmost dimension? We love this as we come. There is a place in amongst it that doesn't falter. Be there, it is true.

Foreign to these places are the needs of thousand wayward nuances. Without thought, nor recompense, we sit beside ourselves, and know which way to turn. There is now a thoroughfare that is distinct. We turn to it in times of trouble.

Blake - Is this what we have known, in simplicity, and in jest? Can we hear ourselves above the tempest? Does the departure come at stages of rest? There are here questions, but do we follow, in times of abandon, times of joy?

A further adventure awaits. One that teems with all the goodness that we can muster. Be that thing than has no sense of it, that has no sense to try any other way. And then, like this, we can glean a further insistence, that will pass the test.

Blake – do you do as we do, climbing on shore walls, reading in public places? There are things we must only do in the presence of greatness. And when the grinding of malt on silver has the chance to listen closely, let it. It will be.

And shall we dance, on unfathomable legs, in trenches as deep as the Nile. There is here a place for pleasantness, and a sighing that weeps for gold. And never in between, shall we be in love like this again. We will fall – we will fall.

Blake – have you seen that pass, that wayward boundary in the sun? There is now a chance for the reckoning of fold, one that is told in fibres of the very marrow. Come and see the quartering of the sky. It will refresh, I promise.

And then, with heart and soul and all the very fibres of what we most hold dear, there comes a chance to climb to the outer rim, and there force ourselves upon fate, and know that in the meantime, life is full of laughter.

Blake – do you know what the remnants of steel remind me of? It is us as we steal ourselves a new life, and then go hunting for the fellowship - where we were taught the art of art. Come and see the closing as we hush ourselves to the middle.

And here, where the moisture is at its lowest ebb – here we see the sense of it, and know things to be true in their centre. I will not care for the whistling in all its tenacity. Feel free, to hearten all that is, with beats of drums that only sparks forth.

Blake – do you see things clearly? Yes you do. The vine is in the vapour that holds the marrow to the gone and the goaded. Do not shine on yellow bends, there can only be the semblance of encounters, and the what for. Please come.

And now, the type of thing we see, is not of the other, nor of the sound. It is of the oasis, and the differing of pounds of togetherness. We need ourselves for what we are. It is because, here, there is no voice of the untamed. But what of love?

Blake – Come to us surely, and then teeter, before rising above. Now, do not retreat, not for a second. Love and embarking. Love and the kind of thing we are trying to prise lose. There are things we have a heart not to do.

My part in this act is not what we expect. It is now for the holding of worn-out acceptances. Mine is the gorgeous coloured one that has as its boldness more than its share of the beholden. Whisper true, density will colour.

Blake – There is more here than the white of garden foolery. Come and see the weathering of tides. Come and be swept away in new and profound ways. There is here, like the rest of it, a new found longing. We will send for it.

A pleasing sense of nothing. One that repartees the sunlight. And then when we found ourselves lost in the time of it, we came for the shards, as they limber ready for the journey. It will come in strides, but not in vain.

Blake – a window unto the soul, that looks as if Pegasus himself could not sit still. But here, where shadows do not creep, the listening of a thousand lullabies dance, and never sit still. We have wandered far, and we will not sit still.

A quarter past the hour! And then, what's more, a sign to guide, and then let be! And then, like a bolt from the sky, a cause to celebrate, and renew. What is heard is not something we should shy away from, but nothing to embrace either.

Blake – is this the spiritual that you seek? Do drums and parting glances see the fibre of the soul? There is still time to depart, before rangers and lonely hearts stop for the renewed. We will come for the day, and stay for the night.

And rounding off our calculations, we see ourselves for the miss-match we truly are. And here, where the silence does not linger – there is everything we have ever wanted. Because here, the stone has not turned to clay. Hay!

William Blake

Blake – do you inspire us, with misty eyes and worn-out glances? Is this where we look? We have the starting passion, but now, which direction is up? We have found ourselves again – but where is that – we do not know!

Being troubled, but being able to overcome. There is here a coda for delay, and a mission for the worthy. Come now, we must not trap the sailor, as he travels from land to land, shore to shore. Time will fashion a new string, sturdy enough.

Blake – does your heart miss a beat, every-time you walk? Does this portent signal what is left? Left of our ease? There is a sense we have that the sating of winter berries will be enough to shake, and enough to bury our old life.

Conscious of a thing. We walk, but where is the distance? We will be on time, but what for? There is like a fledgling that doesn't go along. And here, where the sense of these times remains a mystery, we hold on for dear life. We will travel.

Blake – listening closely. We have come full circle. And here, despite it all, we languish in dreams undreamt. And then, a barrage of whistling arrows, that never know when to stop. I am here, winding in close. There is a harbour we cannot find.

Majestic, and present, the life we led before this is ensconced. And then, without the need to fly again, we travel down the corridors of fate, and be at one with all we see. Come now, we are not forsaken. We only breathe that deeper breath.

Blake – Do you hear what we hear? Are you the same, but different? Can you sense what is here? There are times that have no recourse to the wind. We will find a way through. And when we do, we will never accede again.

There are chances, and then there are chances. We love to steel ourselves for might and bravado, but what of the test, that sings in our ears. What of the test that knows no other vestige. Come know, we must not play truant to the ages.

Blake – Born in 1757! On Broad street! We will never let you go. Now that the hour is here, and time was then. Believe in things again. Believe in the farrowed brow. The thing that draws us through. There are never enough things to paint!

A walk of intransigencies, but one of breath-taking freedom. There are now new ways to be, and new hopes to glean. There is now, and then, all above and through. What do we say, that we haven't said before. A new start, with fresh heals.

William Blake

Blake – The son of a London hosier, you led the perfect literary life. And then, despite yourself more perfect than before. We never stood backwards, only forwards, into that thing called heart – that river that always alters.

And here, we rub down the tirades to a life we should always have led. I know of no other way than this. And here where the sense of the senseless sees only one dimension, we come back to where knowledge hears again.

Blake – you were apprenticed to an artist who worked for the Society for Antiquities. Your luck! And then, when clouds uphold the measuring of being, there remains a time for the greatest adventure yet! Never to wonder on furrowed ground!

There are times, and then there are ways to be. And then in the middle of it all, a majesty that lingers high above. And here, where the sands of mischief ring in the ears of all that is, we come for the tail of it to send us flying.

Blake – you then were admitted to the Royal Academy, and met Fuseli and Flaxman. And then there was the storm, that follows us all. But behind that there was something more, something that had no chance at to begin again.

Hold on, the rites of spring are here, and they tenor in motion to the stars themselves. We will not beg to differ any more, only lessen the blows of fate by the whispering of tiny dragon flies. We will not waste. We will only call-in when asked.

Blake – do we distemper a vagrant heart, until the moors of which never chance? Be careful not to placate the vase, it is of our liking. We have found a friend, the delectable and the kind. Be wary of the nest, it contains the viper and the snail.

A part of the debris we find, is listening in the fixtures. Be a sound ablution to the wind. We will find ourselves there, before things are too late. A mis-match of tumblings see us through to the end. We will find a way.

Blake – are you the spirit that has no recourse to the wind? Do you believe in the way of it, without abandoning yourself? Can you see the sea, despite its grandeur? We will love you for what you are. And then, a fault never arises.

When the sands move, we all move. And when the characteristics of our chosen journeys come together, we pine for the rectilinear motion of it all. Do not be surprised at the bending of tapestries, the come in types of unison.

William Blake

Blake – an ease to fill the void. A considerable delight to maintain the distance. And here we stand once more in the fallow and the cause. I like where you have been. It is not a feeling of camaraderie I seek. I have never kept one to dance. Yes.

When we flitter here and there, we have much more to fight against than the realising of withstanding shadows. And then, I beg of you, do not bend the lead. We have a temperance to feel towards. Be capricious in a mode of light

Blake - There is time, time that we have not thought to exist. And here Blake, we weather the storm, and know ourselves to be sure. There can be no more of this, this rasping for aching on worn out glimpses. Do not see them – they will stop.

And now that things have stopped, and the turning of every wheel has slowed to nothing, there remains a cognition of the frame, that denies the tempest energy to thrive. But here, where we ponder most, there can be nothing other than this.

Blake – is this what there is? Tell a tune, and before it is over, nestle in close. There remains an argument to the contrary, that strikes a chord with the mountain peak. Do only that thing that has as its development the wind – come now, we are in search.

And when we have found it, a tremendous applause will greet us. And here, where the dust never settles, a sign post to the dawn, that constrains nothing, and has nothing dispelled. Be a delight, and the changing of things will reignite.

Blake – are you the one to say, yes, to the daylight? Does this mean only one thing, that your travelling will never cease, and your direction will never waver. We have found a way, through it all, and through it now. Come, do not be displeased.

Come and be at privilege, your star will never wane. What we sense are the whispers in the night, that harbour all that will be. Never once lose sight, and in the code is the trembling of an age. Do not disturb us, we do not tally.

Blake – You went to one of Flaxman's literary gatherings, and sung you poetry aloud. People noticed, as yours was the day, and the semblance of things caught on its own reduction. Hear what you must, you began. And then, again, yes.

All the will, and all the sand, and all that will come to pass, has come to pass. Do not gather yourself in modes of grey, modes of white. Outline was your thing. Stark outline made great art. We will be here for the opening of excellence.

Blake – You had a conversation with Sir Joshua Reynolds, the pre-eminent artist of the day. You weren't happy with what he said, and you remembered, writing about him afterwards in your own way. The dream, and the silence.

Fathoming deep, yours is the wandering, and the feet that are made for walking. Come now, we must not be one to tread on sore toes. We are the listening, as you are the light. Be that as it may, we come for more of the quiet – Yes.

Blake – Your voice was as one in tendrilled harness, and your yoke was taken. Your life began afresh, and your need to be startled by all who took you to be a ranger in a ranger's store. Be the times, as they are you. Define, refine, reschedule.

A feeling we once had, that down at the bottom of things, there is a way, a way forward and through. We have come for the talk, and the feelings of togetherness, and all that will be. Do not treasure us, we do not stay.

Blake – You exhibited at the Royal Academy in 1780. And it was here, that your most ardent passions knew what they should do. There was nothing left, but to follow your own compulsions, through the room, and out the door.

These are tempestuous times, but your times Blake, were also replete with the madness of the world. We come for the seating to a larger crowd. And here, where the dis-ease is never enough to bully. Never enough to say, yes, I do.

Blake – Do we tag along, to places unseen, monuments unknown. There is more of a feeling here. A feeling that doesn't say when, or how, or why. The hope that is here like a shadow in waiting, can never hold forth, nor never relax.

A sort of heart-felt cry, that never unhinges. That much is clear. And what the dandelions snare, is more than their fair share. But here, where we cross paths with neverness, we sound our bugle cry throughout the range. Never stop.

Blake – come to us – let us see you for what you are. There are now the remedies of fate, lifted up strong and together. We carry no other place, than up this ladder, and through this window. Come for the heat of it, as you know.

And then, a half-hearted tiding through it all. We will fight, and fight, until there is no fight left. But what is here, but all that is. What have we gleaned but all the knowledge of the night. Come for the ebb, and the flow will not be denied.

Blake – come for the sense of it, and know it to be a thing devised by love. There is no other explanation. But what of this? This feeling that trudges in pure memory? There can only be the sand that harks its name back through things.

What of this? What of this kind? We never find ourselves free of the moment. And, yes, then, an entrenched soul, one that has as its tail, a feeling right in the middle. And then, without compunction, a sort of riding forth, done in halves.

Blake – cover yourself – the clouds are here for the changing. Never a misbelief, never a traipsing in between. There comes more than this. We will feel our way to the centre, and then give the motion of the sky a holding. Yes.

Considering all, the venting of an age dismisses the call. We will not linger, as in time, nor deduction. But here, where the life we lead is of the second glance, here, the trove of the ancients does not depart, nor head away. Yes indeed.

Blake – do you see yourself in shades and nuances of meaning? Shades and nuances of thought? Should we not be belligerent as the wind takes us? Should we only think one thought, which is up to us? We will transcribe what is here.

Ascending to byways, and through the climb, to nothing left. There are chances to see what is for, and chances to be in tune. With lark in tow, and fire on the embers, there is a mesmerising account of real tenacity. Do not belong – just enthral.

Blake – and now, without temperance, nor invective, there silences a large desire, that came as it wanted, and delighted in the range. There are gusts of wind, that no cloud could pacify. Not here, nor anywhere. Be forgiving, it will attain.

Again, I ask – what of this? This thing that abates and winds, and falls, and lifts. There is nothing to this thing that defies attraction. There is stillness that turns to dizziness, and then away again. We will only learn from fate.

Blake – a softness, we grant you, a softness that does not rise. I am in need of something else. But wait, I have the density of thousand nights labour, gently co-mingling and assorting. These lives we have, entrenched in style, and fun.

A pleasure, a pleasure that resides in the heart. There can only be this, and this only. Whatever may come, will come. Whatever will find its way to garden, will have its share there. There is something different now, but we must not wait.

Blake – 1782, you married Catherine Boucher. In courting her you gave her a small vignette of your life. You then asked her whether she pitied you. She said yes. And you said, "Then I love you." The sea, does it move with inclination?

After this we see a realm that has not lost its feet. We come, and then believe in ghosts, and all the fibre of our books. Come now, we are not ones tell a face from a stranger. Have this thing called love pronounce itself, and not be belittled.

Blake – what is in store for the gauge, and the resolution. How many tried and true examples will afflict the life of it. We have found a way through, and in-between, and around. Never once to find what you are looking for. And then, enliven.

Converging on the right side of the now, the rainswept repartee of tomorrow usurps its place in the sun. Do not be alarmed, there will come a time for the link between this and that. Believe in the time it takes, this much will do.

Blake – after you were married, you taught
Catherine to write and the draw – two important
aspects of your own life. And then a heart as large
as a man comes through in condolences of a
make-shift excitement.

Believing in the fold, we come once again to that
place which is forever untold. And then, when the
sparks of discomfort readily ascend, the makeshift
and the told come in swift succession. Do not love
out of spite. We will have nothing left to give.

Blake – What is left of you? Is it the wind of
commiseration? Is it the pale fibre of the dusk, a
thing we all aspire towards? Does this thing which
shows the way have on its countenance the belief
and need that sings in bellows and chaffs?

Wishing for the sound of the noon-day moon, we
come to that place where the furthest and the best
place themselves in idle chatter. Do not decide on
things irrevocably, there is a chance for inspiration
to raise its beacons taut.

Blake – and then, without the need to wander, a
new kind of silk on press. And it is here that we
find ourselves, not believing, nor condescending,
nor having recourse to the daylight. There comes
a consciousness that lingers in time to the vase.

Concerned, with the heart, and not the soul. There believes a distant chime, one that has not the consistency of the world to endow upon, nor to weep afresh towards. There rings a new set of tears, that which we have yet to understand.

Blake – hold onto yourself, there is more to come. The world is a vibrant place that has as its yoke the seams of another night's distress. And then, without the turn of the dissuaded, much more will come to pass. You never know!

And then, like the dimensions of an out stretched hand, the folly of together being is never heard. We lack what it is that has us as its sail, and us as its sounding board. I love you, and to say that hurts, but the chasm of vibrancy comes through, again.

Blake – do you do all this, in time to a lapse of the hand? The fictitious life you wrote of, will be here again. And now, the readiness that we encumber sets forth, and knows the journey to be one of servitude, and not lassitude.

And then, the heaviness of tomorrow, does us no favours. But in the end, there involves the sort of thing that one wouldn't expect. Laughter, and the sense of more appeal. Do not chose a destination – it will come again forever.

Blake – are you in the lurch? Something to try and understand? And then, a new way – something we don't expect. And here, where the browbeaten, and the cacophonous, merge, long forgotten sallies come to guide us. We will learn a better way.

A simplicity which the sand can only tell of. A new heart we just simply don't have control of. We need something to ponder, and then wait to see what for. The dramatic and the staid, have come here to mind our sense of things.

Blake – Is this the time we hold so dear? Do you regress, when you see the fire in the eyes? Do your tangents appeal to the lonely, and the momentous? Come now, and speak to us. We have the energy left. We want to know, do you love?

Excited by the change. The levity of forbearance distils itself from heaven's tent. And here where the night is like an abandoning, we come to see it in full, and believe once again in faith. There are things we can undo, and things we can do!

Blake – never a time to be in the middle of all this. There is now a multicity of ways against the fervour of it. Do not find yourself alone, the setting

of stone on stone will suffice. And, like a
masquerade, vision is filled to the brim.

There are some things that have as their recourse
the bearing of a load to go by. And then there are
other things that the bearing is for something else
entirely. Never flinch, no matter what. There are
some places we must see.

Blake – A setting of pieces that no longer
warrants the floating down the stream. And then,
the alarm we feel at the most ardent passion. We
have life, now as she should be felt. The massive
underrating of things before we go.

And the washing of the feathers before flight.
What have we thought, but this? What have we
known, but all? What have the tenderest of
charms beguiled? There are times we must only
see once. And then there are only things before
us!

Blake – do you hold a brush as you hold life? With
a gentle confidence that no description entails.
Have the fold in it demolished, and built anew.
There are things that have only sense to guide,
and it is in them, that we are kept asleep.

Lighting the way, we see ourselves in tempest
bloom, that always builds itself anew. There are

foundlings straight, straight through. And here, before we pass, a reticence to be as we like, and do as we please. Not knowing, we come.

Blake – do you detest the morning, that frosts as it cheers? Can there be no greater happiness than at the precipice? Do we long for the ardour of pursuit, and know it to be ours? We have come for the grave – was that Blair's Grave?

Consigned to fate, and then away. You should see us, the misers on the flotilla of the circumference. I have longed for this, as we away from the targets of unusual destination. Come for us, we will travel. And in doing so, harbour.

Blake – a nest of ways, which shall we pick? Blake, do you come in adjacent wares, never hiding, always believing – always crouching, always towards the finishing line. There and beyond. Is that what is there, in the basket of deliverance.

Come for the silence of things, and then the capturing of grammatical inflection. Be nice to us, and come when we seek. There are things we don't understand – but that is okay, we will listen carefully to the waves, and let them know.

William Blake

Blake – we have made it! Through the bramble, and acrid smoke. Through the noise, and the cooling balm. Can we believe in what we want? Does the potion smell of petition? Can we live our lives in accordance to the decree?

Most importantly, we have the wherewithal to marshal our needs towards the very end of things. Come and see the things I see. Come and be the things I have been. Never lustful of steely eyed, always contemplative, and next to assurances.

Blake – do you have the nous? Do you have the sterner stuff? Is this where we go from here – through the thicket and briar, around the bend, in through the window, and out again. Is this what we should do? Such is the mission of us all.

Closing in ourselves. Do we have fight, or flight? Is this enough to go by? Can we never intuit the lives we lead? Come now, for a song, we linger nightly by the grave. What is more the tempest has not its grasp. But what does this mean? We shall see.

Blake, your brother Robert was living with you, and while there, he passed away. You said you saw his soul ascending to heaven. The sea – the rush of it. Pounding life, abundant. What the sea doesn't contain. We will never know.

Safety in the trees, and then a long set for numbers. We will tail the wind, but for what purpose? We have never known the way of it, only that which is partial in dimension. Come and be the wind for a time, we must willow in amongst it.

Blake – an unknown delicacy wavers in the breeze. Have your salt, as I have my sugar. Hold on, there is no time left. Hold on, a draft in the windows of things. Ill-spent, but mischievous. What we have not found in any place other than this.

A fortunate invigoration, that dispels as it departs – have you found the key? The key that unlocks the door? There is something here for all of us. In inertia we find something that gives us more. In motion, we are like the wave. Yes, and above.

Blake – beholden to the stars – evaporate unto the noon. Bespeckled unto the mystery, and then to rise again. Never relished, but only in stride. Give the Caesar up, and have it fold down. What do we see when life is tough – Many things.

A new thing, seen only once, in the history of it. Never wandering through, only at delight. Squeeze the life out of it, and have it settle back into rhythm, nothing like the cold to bring out the best in us. And here, before we are gone, sabres to rattle.

William Blake

Blake – do you have a miniature to do? Something commissioned? We are here with you. Be the lingering calm, and the state of finery will be yours. Do not forget one thing or another! Just believe in yourself, and the night-gate will be open to you.

Gaining in sand moved. We no longer arch our backs for the sense of it. We hear something now that has never been heard. And we rejoice, rejoice at the simplicity of it! There is a bastion here, that levies all who want!

Blake – do you slavishly wander through the mists? Is this where we can find you? In touch with so much. There resigns a tubular shape that has the now as the solstice. Be forever here – we do not belong without the consciousness on the reef.

Amongst the debris, there stands a statue to it all. And here, where we send our most ardent passions, we see ourselves through veins of arcane wisdom, that only know themselves to be true. And this is now it, a wonder, and a furthering.

Blake – do you have the listening of a knowledge untold? Is it you that balances on cups of gold? Can we find no other way but you? Hush, we must think, and study, and be what the wise man has told us. Now then, back to it.

A fashioning of something precious – a testament to the rose bush. A heart in amongst the thistle. There is a sound here, one we have not heard of in a long time. But what we say is enough, when to be enough never grows.

Blake – I am with you, Blake. I lead a party of ten. I have no need for the tendrils of it all. But what I do have, is the foundation stone to a vast citadel. Here I will lie, until lying is enough. Come now, we must not depart. We will continue until all else.

Leaving us with more to do. There is a chance here that all will mend. There is a chance here that prying hearts and prying ways are enough to sell our syncopated dream to the world. Do not believe otherwise. There will be time. Just wait.

Blake – hanging on for life. Being made of steel, and then transpiring to the rafters. I am one to see things clearly, and in this a tale is told. A tale that we never thought possible. And then, with gracious acclimatising's of silk on hard won sweat, verity.

Causing more than a stir, the little time we have left is enough for us to say our piece, and have our right to the stars re-aligned. Do not be so sure of yourself, not here where the ferry of life does not stop for anything, nor anyone.

Blake – Hanging on to all around you, whether here, or there. Come in for a closer look, and see things as they are. There is a chance that we can look assuredly, and without ropes. Running through things, that is the best way to go.

Holding things down in the rough sea, we imagine with outstretched hands what is here to engage with. And then in the way of it, a sense of calm, to right the ship, and have it sail high on the water. Come now, we must not be dismissive.

Blake – To be treasured like you are, but not left to be, to sing, nor to gurgle. There are times that we feel at home in the world, and times we don't, but it is here that we feel more than ever. Do not be shocked at what you see, there is time to be.

A belief, that out-weighs to the bending of the light. And here, silence in the winter of our hearts. Never be one to shirk – always continue with fresh spirit, and light boots. A sort of thing we could never miss. Always be strong, it will help.

Blake – to our hearts, and to our hands, we feel this journey of yours, as a time watched thing. Do

not be surprised if the tenacity of winter's night
rolls into the dust. There is fight here, that drowns
out the noise of life. Be calm, it will suffice.

Come laden weather, there is no need for the
hoary frost never to depart. There is now a certain
space in the distance between our heart beats.
Come now, do not dispose of the density of it – it
is needed down the line.

Blake – a sort of courage we rarely see, in
amongst the fitness of the ball. There comes a
seeing – a seeing into things – something that has
not been there from the beginning. We ruffle our
feathers, and now that time will not depart.

A sort of lullaby, one that is reminiscent of the
card. To say yes, is not to deny love. To be there,
at the right time, is to be an anchor in a sea of
doubt. Be the way we dance, and there will be a
netting of things untold.

Blake – You described that way you wrote as
'dictating from the spirits' – sometimes 30 lines at
a time – sometimes even against your will – You
described writing a long epic poem, that seemed
like a work of a long life, but was in fact no effort at
all.

William Blake

A sort of route that we rarely see, but have come to know and respect. Come now, do not relinquish the need of it, there is here like a rain on tin rooves. The feeling we have for each other is nothing short of attuned. Do not say, only see.

Blake – a lingering in amongst us. There are things we must push ourselves for, but somethings not. And then, like a talon in the night, a sort of release that doesn't bend the day. Do this once, and the force of it will not chafe.

Sitting there, not moving. Allaying our fears, but for this. A tremendous wind, comes at us from the tenderness we all feel. We all feel this at life, but what of the sand, that comes in unison with the thread? We know not how to explain.

Blake – there are things that have as their adversary the chiming of winter wolves. And here, where the division between this and that is more than we can sew, there lies a painstaking afront, that believes itself a stranger, but is a land unto itself.

Tempting to some, and not to others, there is a sense that translates into nonsense, and a fallacious need to step on stones. We have won a mighty battle, in front of it all, to times of laughter, and times sanguine ease. Be ready, it will come.

Blake – Do you sell your work with gusto – in between the mansion and solstice? Is there a time to be beautiful in an ugly place? I will follow you unto the glacier, and the many spotted land. I see your heart, and know it to be pure.

Ungainly, and with repute. There sings a tree in a place of refinement. But here, where the leaves of autumn fall, they are gathered by the hands of Los, and scattered over vestiges of land so far unseen. Yes, we will ride.

Blake – have nothing to say, and yours will be a harlequin dismissal. And then the tables turn in on themselves, and the walking stranger limps over the munificence of the daylight. We are here to climb to another ladder – and then across and through.

Forms of heavy rainfall spring eternal from the shelf. And here, where the mistletoe knows no indulgence, we come again to the light of things. It is as if we heard the sail unfurl, and thought to ourselves, how can we be in this?

Blake – is this where we go? To the top of everything? The mound is steep, but what of the song? Treasures are hidden, but what of the pan-flute? There is in us a need to try, and be attuned to love before we say good-bye.

Urizen, your nemesis, trying as we might to let go of things enough to see the end! There are things we do not see, end-points and starting points. Do this thing, where noise erupts in larder tones. We are near then, but far.

Blake – do you see the way through, and then evasive? Is this what we say, in chariots of wheeled tomorrow? There is now a sense we can do the thing which afflicts us. And now, tremendous stars burst in fiery wonderment. We will see!

Seeing ourselves double, and then in the meantime happiness. Do not draw on the gist of it – there will be no time. Come to the restful slumber of it all – despite the stallion that takes us there. Believe in what you will, the answer will come.

Blake – do you say to yourself, look, there is no clearing, there is no way through. But these are merely impossibilities. We can do what we like with them. There is no means which denies the formal and the irreproachable. Never stop.

Looking forward, we see in the distance the mist of another time. This mist, that does not grow, is likened to a gumption that speeds along the path like a plough after the harvest. And then despite it all, a new wheel to mend – and then…?

Blake – holding on like never before, being-in-the-midst of it all, and feeling great. What is this thing we see before us? Is it the sample of the tree and wood? Is it the rite of dandelions that have spring as their moisture? Come, let us see!

A new way to be, one that doesn't wander forth, nor surprise the autumn of its leaves. Come and see what is near, and what is far. We have the right of things to bury in the depth and see ourselves anew. Do not find the way through, it trembles.

Blake – having a grasp of it, and seeing it catch. Having more than what is at stake, and dreaming of the tiles of it. There is nothing more than can be said of it. To take the lead, and have it burrow. There is only what can be said.

Openness to what is around us. There is now the time it takes all things. We have not lost heart, and drag ourselves through the last gate as if the moon would shine one more time. There is here enough the tendency to cry. Yes.

Blake – do you love as you see? Do you reckon on glances made of cake? Is this where we know ourselves to be? In lands unwary, and in places unwrapped, there is something more to see, something more to understand, something more to say.

Do we sound the bell on the rocks of disbelief? Or do we gather ourselves for another forest walk? There are things we must do, and things we shouldn't. But what is left is in the middle is all that should be. Come now, we must not part.

Blake – sensing the mystery, the time it takes us is enough to whittle away the hours of a long-lost bravado. There comes a sound down the halls, that listens intently if we let it. There is more that can be salvaged, in one way or another!

Jostling for position, the way we go about things is enough to sally-forth in identical numeracies. Please do not go, I have many plans for the two of us. We will play at the theatre, and know we are having fun. And then when we are done - silence.

Blake – having the sense to just be for a while. Having what is at stake, until the freshness of reality no longer bites. Blake, do you see the stars? Do you wander further than ever before? Is this where we turn, to you? I believe in you.

Coming together like a tether on dry wood. There is in this formulation something that smarts, and also, that uplifts. Come now, do not be dismissive, there rises a chance at something. Be the sentinel, and life will come forwards.

Blake – are you conscious of the need we all have to water the sea with our tears, and send longing into straights of the narrow? If so, please do come in! And then, when the dust has fallen, and the ground is like a receiving pole, we will shape!

Come now, do not bemuse the subject, or its matter, there are things that we have not to do, and things we must do rightly. And in these things are the sun and the moon, and the stars, and everything to revolves in the sky. Yes, again.

Blake – come in from the cold, the tempest delights here. I know of nothing to stop us in our journey to the centre, but the centre of this place is nothing we can count on. Be the tribe, and all will be with you. Be a safe harbour, and saying will ease.

Do not ascribe consciousness to where it is not needed – but do where it is! That is all I can say, you must determine for yourself, where things are right and things are wrong. Only believe in what you think, and then have some fun.

William Blake

Blake – Fastening on with great resolve, we gather ourselves for one last bridging forward. And then, with our minds set, we travel instantly to where we want to go. But what is there to do now? Nothing but reach in the orchard of things.

And now we understand – the thing we miss the most, is the same thing we had all along! But what of us now, now that the mist is ready to disperse? Now that the sea has been drained, and all that is left is the heart and soul of things?

Blake – do you sample the rainfall in all its forms? Do you never placate things without nous? Is this what we say when we are rushing? Never believe in the tailor until the mass is given. Always sing past the hour, but never through it.

Arching our backs to run that little bit faster. Having a hold of the daylight so that it never escapes. Being scared, but not turning away. Being close to things like we always wanted. Being away with consummate ease. Come, there is sense.

Blake – Thomas Butts, your great patron, paid you a visit – he arrived at your abode, to find you and Catherine inside naked, quoting Milton's Paradise Lost to each other! All you said was – "Adam and Eve here". Ha!

Sensing what is next, through the fibres of it all. I have come here to rest on the cobblestone of life, never to lose, always to guard. And here, where pain is like a fair journey, we will discover how things move, and come to be.

Blake – so kind, and in shape, always moving, always winding – a kind of nuance that lingers in the way of the pride of your existence. There can never be a soul more worthy of this! This that we bestow upon you. Further through than ever.

Something in the middle of the road, that moves away with the right sound. And here, where we live the most, there carries with us a certain calm, that mitigates the sound of disquiet in the changing of the guard. Come and be placated.

Blake – a tenacity that doesn't waver. Something in the wind that has nothing to stop it. And then, like birds in flight, a feeling that was once here but not remembered. I will lie-down for you, and have my name etched in sorrow. There is nothing but this.

Considering where we have come from, this is a good result. But this is the stage where we are at. Come now, fire and ice do not beckon, nor do they recall, nor sing, nor post lullabies. The world is a lullaby, without the comfort, nor the sound.

Blake – the difference in temerity between this hill and the next, shows what the daylight is made of, and then wisps of other worldly pleasures, from different spheres if you will. There comes a time for action, and a time for contemplation. Be still.

A bread basket that has air as its companion. I have seen what is right, and what is wrong – coming first, and coming last – being tangential, and sending his far. This is the way it happens, so let us rejoice, and have a play on words!

Blake – there was once a well-meaning man, who had no time to fill. His most ardent passion was that of the ball. But when he came through, his job was done. He had no time for the sense of the night, and in that he commissioned no stances.

A busyness to uphold, that governed no might, no tenure, no uplifting to the light. Come and see it through with us. The science of it is right. But here Urizen waits, does he not, but we must cast forth and see our bronze a gold.

Blake – the start of something special, that does not waver. We tread down as if by motion itself. And that is the best way to describe it. The telling of the wolves, we list by age and number. There is more than that which we have come to.

Much-of-a-muchness - when it comes down to it. Furthermore, harps sing when we lay indulged. Do not come in times of feather, nor in reams of afterthought. There is this and only this. And here we laugh, laugh at it all.

Blake – we see you in the afterglow, of worn-out places and worn distempers. I have found something in you, that maybe you regret, but that is okay. And then when sweeping streets comes to be norm, we will once again be in time with things.

Reaching back in regards to time, we have as a presence the need of far-receded lives. And here where the things we do follow strictly from the corner of the room, we tell ourselves that life is garnished, and that the things which carry us, carry all.

Blake – catching all there is to catch. Hoping for the delight of May, and where we are led to. There is much to be said here, much to be done – so let us do it, before it is too late. We have never known a moment like this.

William Blake

Delighted to see you in, delighted that we came back. There is now a chance at skittles, and all that lives. Be the one who triumphs, and the stark metal will not spark. Catching a harbour beyond the pale of a doubt. We will see it through!

Blake – standing firm to the core of things. Having a bushel to carry, but not caring. There is here wanderlust that knows itself to be true, and in tune with all that is. Coming to the inkling of the station in turn, we love what we see.

A spearing glance, that has as its compulsion all the lives of the sea. In between all this, what is more, there is a love that beats on rowdy drums, and has as a sailor raw courage, and little bits of land to give. And then, sense amongst the rubble.

Blake – a solace in the wind. Something too good, but there. And when the rain falls, it doesn't stop. Like this vessel, that knows no harbour, but yet keeps moving, and moving and moving. Never once have we thought of it, to be this, and this only.

Half in the strangeness of it, half in its aplomb. Do we envisage time to be a yoke, or a freedom to explore? We do not know, only that the treasure of the night is born of a mighty number. Shed itself in true grandeur, and then fixate to the willow.

Blake – we are in, and having quite the time.
There are memories to tame, and visages to
claim. And in this there comes more to the front
than we could have imagined. Be quiet, we will
simply go our way. Simply.

And here, where the sun shines in colours, there
remits an hour to be told. And in this, we feel a
southern chance, a chance to be as we are, and
stand before history as a someone who bit the
sinews of fate. We will see ourselves coming
again.

Blake – are these all that we have found? Are
these the same as the pouring way? Never come
here for breakfast, we hear of our tutelage in the
foreignness of it all. Never believe in the way of it.
There is much to be said for the articulation of
things.

There is here, something we don't understand,
and cannot grasp. And in this, the way of all things
is expressed. And here, we delve a little deeper
into our lives, and then look up, and see that
things have not the roll of the dice. Yes, but some.

Blake – we sound ourselves out such that the
times do not tarry. And in the more of it, a sense
that daylight doesn't matter – and all that does

matter is the sequence of events of here to there, and around again. We will never leave.

What is it we have found? It has something of the ease about it. And here, where the tonic, the elixir of life, is discovered, we remember ourselves, and have as a wanting bliss a sense that never fails. Come now, we will find ourselves a new track.

Blake – do you compromise? Or is this your last approach? Do you have as the wand, a keeper of sorts? Is this what we say when the trickle becomes a torrent? I am wishing for the tribulation to continue. This much cannot be said, it is sure.

There are places where the mist does not rise. There are things that cannot be seen, until they are seen. And here, where the life blood of an age continues, we will remember what it is that keeps us ticking.

Blake – to have as heaven and earth the ground itself. And as it parts, a new sense of what it means to be alive. We do not see much past our own eyes. Come now, in sequence, we evolve, and come to transition to the night. Here and again.

And then, without the thought to be any different, there belongs a cry that willows the sentient charm

– well before us. And then, despite our signature, there is a sound in the attic that resembles all that is. We come for this sound. It is our anchor.

Blake – I sense your away-wardness is not a problem – but what makes us stand, is not the continuation of a blur, but something much more insightful. Be much to those who have the semblance of life – there's is a mighty journey. Come and sing.

What is this I see – a sight that amazes, as it tires. There is something that we must not see, and in that the sight seems even more amazing. Come now, only give in to satellite wishes, and most ardently, all that will delight.

Blake – most treasured, feathers, and willing grace. There are things to do, to make a home a home. And then, like never before, starlit wonder, and a piece of the unusual. We are not lost in the forest. Far from it. We revel in the journey.

A feeling we once had, but have no more. Shreds and heights we simply don't feel. But what we have is a teleology, and vice regal desire, and all that will come to pass. And in this we are happy, if not a little harried.

William Blake

Blake – sensing the mystery of it! Being prey upon by wonder. There is a likeness to the sky – an open expanse. And when we have found ourselves again, here we sing the tune of hope, and have it send ourselves through once more.

Having the ritual to be not too reluctant. And here, where the shine of the bastion never relinquishes, there is a sound that only we can hear. And then, like magic, things appear and disappear, and go through the ages in the most simplistic way.

Blake – holding still, we never hold our breath for too long. But wait, what is that here? This thing that burrows in deep? There is now a long-entrenched repartee that believes in rest as it believes in strength. What have we here? More than enough.

A vast array of things to see around. Do not come unless you are bidden. Do not have what you should not. Be the one to not wither on the vine, and we will come to you in your greatest hour. Be soothed, the arch will triumph for its shape.

Blake, a reminiscing of times gone by. A short approach to a difficult problem. There is now nothing left, nothing left of the ball. This is sacrosanct, as is all of life. Do not change for anything or anyone. There will be enough time for that at the solace.

A wish that hurries us, a chance to do things right. And when we find our distance, we will conquer more than the wind. Do not deliver us unto the trees of the forest, we will not go. And here, where we are invigorated in our opposition, we laugh, and play.

Blake – do you run, a great distance, and see yourself believing in things to come? Are you the one never to recite an adage from the tears of suggestion? There are things in the wind that only lie down after a day of solitude, and rest.

And roundabouts, through, and with vigour, we know our destination, so let us commence. It is here that have not seen the daylight for all of two days. But what is this anyway, nothing but a spark to the necessity of things. We will come.

Blake – are you the one to see us through? Is this what we do, to un-trench the heart? Can there even be another way? Can the dimness of the round settle us, like a navigation sent to right. Only here do we see. Only here do we truly placate.

Anonymous and central, speeding through the way. I have never seen a chance like this. It is here in the rainbow, that we creep forward, and know ourselves to be true. But then, without a thought, we sense something new. What is it? – it is us!

Blake – ending the conundrum, we frolic where we need to be. Close to where this is, is the stairwell to the stars. Leaping up – "I have been you, I have seen you!" There is nothing now to concern the sports of fantastic endeavour. Be real, it will suit.

Afternoon of the well-spring, I see things clearly. I have never felt such camaraderie for the suitability of the journey. What is left is all that can be. What is here, is the flight into neverness and beyond. Do not curtail yourself, there will be more.

Blake – a having as a regression to be. And when the moment strikes us, we feel ourselves lifted to some other place, and some other time. What is this place, what is this time? Much fair repute ruffles on these pinions. We will still.

Having the need we had exhausted through and through, we launch into the environs of delectability, and have as our wish the times that do not beckon. Love and solitude, two poles in the scheme of the world. We will never miss.

Blake – are you the one to see straight? The one to feed the dozen skies, and to hear the masterstroke as it occurs. Be sure of yourself, you are in control. A little bit of time is all we need to transform this straight into thunder – we will.

Going on, despite the migration. Saying please, in short to dine. There are noises in the dark, that do not feel for us. But despite everything, there is nothing like this, expression in the wind, up against the folly to continue. We will never stop.

Blake – giving things, and wishing for the light. Having more to say, and then saying it. And here, where the tempest is all we have, we will be mindful of the rest. Come now, there is nothing more to do, nothing more to feel – you will see.

Having things to take delight in. Being a passenger in an amazing ride. And then, like a score in charge, there remains more than the fibre of things. There is here, like the rest of it, a sempiternal glow. Do you see? Do you see? I hope!

Blake – assuredly, things will change. Assuredly, the manor will remain the same. But here, where the furthest cry unbuckles the night-swift, there comes a chance to redeemed things. What can we say that has not been said? We will find a way.

In motion, and through thought, we carry ourselves off to that place in the thousand abodes, and have as our time the whispering of fate. And then, despite the hungriness of the journey, we relay ourselves in full. Communique!

Blake – what assuredness is this? What has the gull brought in, that does not opine the relic? Come now, and hope we last from this point to the next. There is nothing like this, the sand on tongues of steel, and forging on scorched memories.

Hanging on, for this or that. For this parchment, or that delight. And here where the sounds of our teeth chattering is enough the wake the dead, there is more now than the sun can abide. Be a ritual in a ritualistic land, and your fight will ease, to be sure.

Blake – You couldn't get a soldier out of your front garden. He later said that you had said – "Down with the King, down with his soldiers, down with the populace". You where charged with High Treason!

Rounding out the sense of it, we find ourselves questioning things about the nature of the sky, that is in keeping with the hard reliances to come. Do not feel wrath here, the life is up for the tempest, and is nothing more than can be sampled through.

Blake – you were asked to pay 250 pounds in bail.
You defended yourself, and at each time the
soldier said something you thought was false, you
simply cried out "false". You won the case, and
return to London in victory.

A nice touch, the plaque on the wall. Gives your
home that homely feel. And here where the clouds
never cease, the glass that gathers winter rain,
has more to say than the winter of our joy or frost.
Come now, forever in spring. Forever.

Blake – a movable time and place; an orchestra
of minds – something to think over. What is the
time of it, that comes in short sense and
delipidated style. Come to be the agreeable, and
the lonesome in you will fight again.

Jasmine and rose petal – something to make a
room out of. And here, where the libations of an
age no longer settle, we do not cancel the dance,
for anything, or anyone. There is motion here, and
it is forward. Yes, in threes!

Blake – a patron for you! And all who care to
pass. There is something chimed in the well – and
here where dozens pass daily, there is meaning in
the waters of it. Come now, we must not let
ourselves linger. We must see what comes to
pass.

William Blake

Nothing but the sleight of hand. Nothing but
stillness where we have walked. The time it takes
to walk a mile is the same time it takes to write a
book, given we see things the same, and in-line.
And then there is tempestuousness – we see it.

Blake – have we the circumference of the thing?
Do you feel the wandering is full of nectar, that
has nothing of the wraith, and all of the triumph?
There can be nothing more than this – to be at the
vanguard of fate, and letting ourselves be!

Feeling like the thing we thought was past, has
come back in arching deliverance. And here,
where we look for the tide of it, a new sense that
comes in the mode of happenstance. And now,
with a flurry, there is a reason to be. Here we
come.

Blake - have you found the staff to your liking? Is
this what we live for, to range over field and hay,
and sense that the noise will be enough to sooth?
There is here a merriment that cannot be shook.
Come for the tension of it. It will suffice.

Gold, and taut replies. Witnessing, but with what?
There is like so much of the transposition here, we
cannot find the path for the stairs. Have the mild of
disuse come forward, and the thing we thought
was a misnomer will be enough to placate.

Blake – Is your tact a folly in the chime of it? Does your reading of it hang like spice, ready never to fly? Come for the dice, but stay for the slumber. There is now nothing left to the sky, and here, where we know ourselves as free, what left?

A great thing, a great thing. What is cautious, is now forbidden. What is now of the order of it, is high on the plateau, where dreams are fashioned out of silk, and the marsh that keeps us is thrown aside, and what is of life, commences.

Blake - what do you do? How do you say? What does it sound like? There is a sense we all have that the right way to bustle into life is through the door of our choosing. And here, where the moisture of life is rich, we will find things to our liking.

Another round of life – what next, could there possible be? What next could we possibly see? There overcomes all eventualities, in this, as in then, as in when? There has now been no cycle to love, and none to ride forth, or have with.

Blake – a stare that no longer hinders. A mismatch of colours that are always worn. There is now a sense that the time it takes is enough to unfurl the flag of abandon, and have as a non-stultifying effect on an inspiration of the heart.

And yet, we cannot see – we cannot ride, we cannot dance the dance of life. But what do we know of, when to know is like a window on the soul? The distance between me and you is nothing more than mischief would have.

Blake – do you hope to dream, and hope to say your last rite? There is more in the stars than we have sought for. And now, where the invigoration of an age only fills half the void, there is an arc that belittles as it carries. Come, we will see.

The best, in rainbow hues, the best, in transfiguring what should not be. And then, without cause nor reason, a new handling denounces the where-with-all, and all that shall pass. What is this thing, I hear you ask? It is never a bridle to a bridle song.

Blake – a sea that doesn't sink. A tree fall that cushions on the way down. And here where nice and ambient rules the nest, we see ourselves again in the way of things to come. Be not intrusive, we are here to do your bidding. Come now, be kind.

An armistice in what is now supposed. A handling
that delves deep. A costume that reveals more
than it hides. And here, where the lacquer has its
time in the snow, we love everything that we see.
Don't belittle the sun, it has come for us.

Blake – do you see the clouds? Do they move in
your fashion? Is this what a turn of speed can do?
Do we like to say more than is due? Have the
ocean at your beck and call, and what you will find
will stop a nation. Be ready, in this is your life.

Looking onwards, we see ourselves in blue-green,
and pale water colours. Is this what we say to the
wind? Is this what the wind says to us? Coming up
for air, we give everything a wide birth. What is
this we say, that doesn't hope to change.

Blake – what does your sense say, Blake? What is
the smoothness of the transition from night to
day? What can only be a more entrenched view of
the way things are, and things are not. Do not
send art Blake, it is wanted elsewhere.

A hedging that litters the way. What is felt, and
what is forlorn. We whisper our regrets in tunnels
of some magnitude, and here finds some
reticence. Do not linger in the cove, there are
spices left, left by the forefathers of yore. Come for
the depth.

William Blake

Blake – there is a peak, that listens to all who come. And on that peak, there is a distance, that harvests all the dreams of all the people. And here, where niceties acclaim, there finds an outlet for all the world – it is all measured, for want of less.

Acclaim, and circumstance. Believing in things as they come. Seeing the water in the desert. Being acclimatised to disappointment. What is there left, but the ridges of fortitude. We will sing a new song, before anything else has eclipsed us.

Blake – we are tearful, and without remorse. What has the daylight given us, but the shine on feet of random wear. Never before has this been so close, so close to runners of fibre yawned. There is here a frankness that defies, all that is.

A harbour that knows when to settle, and when to go. All the ships in the sea wish to be there, without the need to wish. There is something we wish to say – and that is, in the mist, everything seems softer – everything appears grey for the first time.

Blake – are you aware of the goings on of fate? Is this what we have told you not to be in and through? Come now, the fibres of love that you have encountered are not your own. You have borrowed them from the night sky, and know them to be plenty.

A sister to the Blake – we can only insist for next time. And then, without the carrot or the stick, we love what it is that keeps on guessing! Be a trial, and yours will fade on the line of non-passioned. We love this, and cannot let go.

Blake – there are hands that send ourselves to nights of elongated distress. Much have we come for. Much have we seen in the meantime. I was listening once to the sense of it, and I bespoke more than what is possible. Here we go then!

Aroma and the need to stop. Catching the fibres of all that is. I have wished for things of a far-reaching nature, but this is what is best. The creation of words – and in the sky, a change, I have sensed it, and will accommodate.

Blake – do you envision the likeness to the wind, as she tendrils through the day, in vastly escalating numbers. Do not give up – this much is clear. Do not give up, to anyone, or anything. The soul of this is written in these pages. We will find a way.

The after effect of the noise of the spheres is a stoic one at that. There can only be shortfalls

William Blake

where there was a dilemma. There is here, a head to the well-spring, that knows only hope. Give if you like, this thing, where food never flounders.

Blake – have you seen more than you can see? Is this where the road leaves you? Can we fathom more now than ever? Yours is not for the loss of things. Yours is only for the gain of things. And what is more, we love a challenge. How can we not?

A sometimes gathering, of the likes of literary minds – you went to many and here, you staked your claim. What is there now but treasures of inspiration still floating. Come now, there are places we must see, and if the time is right, love.

Blake – did we hear more than the repartee? Is this a thing of grace, that to course through, there must be no boundary. And then, despite ourselves, there is a course of action that is quick, and to the fore. Love the stance, it is here to come.

Forever lingering by the fireside, being worthy of the finish line. There are times we do not see. There are places we have a feel for. Coming to us, is exactly the way we want. There can only be one direction. And that is through, and through.

Blake – send your ships along, do not send them around. There is a chance today, that we will heal all wounds, much to the strongest, and to the weakest. There can only be one result from here, and one result only.

A fashionable delay, one that holds hope. Do not tarry for the length, it hurts when we are not there. And when a deed is done, that harbours no weight, there holds the repercussions of an age. Never mind the fixing. We have turned.

Blake – furthest from our mind, is the turnstile of desire, and when we are eclipsed, we will follow in our own footsteps, and there will be more to celebrate, than to wish in the new year. Do not feel secure in the way of it? There is here a way forward.

An image close to our hearts. A painted head, which causes no grief. There is now a time for reflection that gives solace as it gives a reminder of things to come. Do not steal the soul of it. That is a priceless part of any person, or anything.

Blake – a sense we have that the night will not encumber our shore with any new furrows. And then, a light that burns brightest, comes for the rite of it. Do not tarry any longer, further, or in-between. There comes a dark abyss – no, no longer.

William Blake

Beginning again, we hold forth with the touch-stone of fore-thought. And then, like a rod gone astray, there relinquishes a hold on the breadth of it. And now, without anything to pull us back, we come full circle, and know our life to be invigorated.

Blake – do you hear, my friend? Do you sense the striding forth? Is this what we need, time's elapse? There is a certain kindness in the way of it. And here, where the need to be outweighs the drive to speak aloud – we are there.

And here, a sign to the folk who do not live in twos. There is much more to say here, much more to do. A second minute to fashion a life. Come now, we are at the traipsing door, all the more covered, we cast aside the rain, and feel things again.

Blake – absorbed, and absorbing. Do you sometimes think of yourself in those terms? There is here a wrestling of angels – to be said. And then, with a far cry, something more descends – what is this, that wallows in search of comfort?

Catching the way of it – soothing into milk and delight. There is here a new fashioning of old guards, that if followed, will lead to our seeing anew. Do not be surprised if the sands turn rough, and the merriment of the sky sees us through.

Blake - the signs we digress are written in the spheres. Only a night-time exploration of the sky will attest to this fact. And then, with the sort of feeling we had as children, we launch into life, never to be remedied. Come now, it is all for us.

The sense we have that the twilight is more than an aggregate of lost time. And here, where the measure of a person stacks up in pairs, there is a frost covered reticence to be overcome. But that is fine, to be who we are, we will not change for anyone.

Blake – do you come in stages? Do you feel as one? There is now a sense that the rose bloom has a nectar all of its own. Do not fetch the lonely, they are not in need of help. And here, where we whisper the names of the living, future plans, and life!

Harbouring the mist. Having a time of it. And when we are there, we will know this to be true. The things about which we fathom our delight, know no other way. Considerable approbation, and limited distraction. Come now, we must sing.

William Blake

Blake – the very fibres of the world are here – here to be revelled in. What is more we have here a salutation to the sky, and all she will bring. There is now a chance for the urbane in us all to flourish. And when we are there, might and peace.

A flight of cormorants. We see them, as they dash across the sky-line, and know them to be birds of great wonder. There is not a heart-beat missed, nor a flourish let faded. What we have is something special to wind onto, and through and beyond.

Blake – do you see yourself in pale colours, in shawls of grey, and whites of the April sun. Do not forget this. Do not have as the moat a roundabout way of saying yes. There climes on the two of us much to discuss, and much to do.

Reminiscent of the noon, there comes into view a ruined abbey, with only one person living there. These are mighty times, with mighty robes of red to thread us. Does the dream to have still, still a part of us? I believe so.

Blake – a delicious treat, something we would have as children. And there in the daylight, a sense of what is to come. There can be only hard-work, chiselling the stone away – life as a sculpture by one of the greats.

Wandering far and wide – we settle into our rhythm, to say the least of those distractions. They do not bother us though, and even if so, our gallantry knows no bounds. Have the wind beneath us, and we will travel further than ever.

Blake – a little twist, and all that remains is life. A simplicity of forever. Knowing when to stay, and when to go. Holding on such that we never fall. Are you Blake, the one who follows? Is this where we draw our line, in the sand, and in freedom?

Entertained before us. We will never take the right road - only this time. A ridge that has no folly, and no desire of its own. There is a mighty recourse to the dreams we have, and had, and that is to hold the witness by the hands, and simply do.

Blake – are you one to linger at the base of the hill, always to start your approach late? It doesn't matter, but what we say, is to commence. And here where the disastrous meets the lake, there is a chance to catch a sight unseen.

Further from the gist of it than we know. And here, where the rag-pile and the daylight know their lot, a sense that that the waning of the light is always in check. Verily, and in need of the shadow to fully be, there is here the way of it.

William Blake

Blake – a miniature to be made – something more to talk about. A new way to lose ourselves in the dimensions of it. Come for the trail within. A scent we have, and cannot let go off. Over ripe, but having the same taste. We will sing for it.

Gaining in stature, there is a new way to be. But what we have found, is the old way is best, best for a number of reasons. But one is comfort, the other is fairness, and then there is hope, hope of a life well-lived. Do not fear, we are here.

Blake – are you one to travail? For your personal goals? Do you feel the statues feet? Is this where we commence? In our entirety, and in our new view. There is a sort of thing that is unexplained, that we must traverse. Come now, swim!

Are you the sea, as close to the land? Is this what you see all around you? Do you listen closely to the water, gleaning searchings, searchings only for you and me. Is this what we say, when times are difficult, and in need of respite.

Blake – are you the well-spring from which it came? Is this what we see before us, an origin of water? There can be no other way! Stay strong, we will not let in pain. Are you the object of our choice? Do we hear things again clearly? We must wait.

A fever pitch – something new, to round out the old. Is this what we seek, avenues of desire? Can we be forward in a forward land? Much that we say is rounded, with accompaniment. But despite all we say – windows are for looking.

Blake – does the rain come down here in sheets – sheets of buoyancy? Are you one to reign in the lay of it? And here where the times are vision filled, we see what the tenacity of all things is like. Do not disturb us – we will come.

A sentience that excites. A science in the way of it. Nestle in close, close enough to spark. There is a tremendous wave here, going forward and backward. Something we did not foresee, but have time to tell about. Launch in, do not renege.

Blake – are you strong enough to last? Does your commission fly through to the spring? Is this what we mean when we say "stranger". All the more, a collection of ribbons that show the way – do not depart, there is here room to move.

A new sense we have, to tailor the old. Forgive not the trojan's horse, it comes to take. Be in style, the life we lead can be nothing other, and here where the firefly is not of this sphere, we come to see things again, and have some fun with life.

Blake – There occurs a curious image in our imaginations – we do not doubt it, but when we are resting it is there. Oblong shape, with square base, colour – green of the trees. We will test its worthiness to be in us, and then allow it be there (or not!)

A vision, what's more, using the eidetic in us. And here where the life-blood of our search, comes in full swagger, we jump forward, and see ourselves running to catch up to life. Once we have caught it - what then? We marshal our dreams, and move!

Blake – a heart-felt release from the doldrums. There is further to go, but what of the now? We will be at an ache to be here longer. And then, with the chase behind us, there comes a time for relaxing, and feeling without guard.

And then, without the need to be in tune, there relies on the fabric a measure of solemnity, that brings an oath to bear. And here where dreams mingle with the light of it, a new belief tingles with alacrity. Do not swallow the water, call a truce.

Blake – a feather in the style of it, and then, I hear you say, what style is that? – It is our style, as we lunge once again into the might and fro of all things. There is a tension here that relies on the most of it. But do not say one thing against us.

There is a way forward, as there is a way back – but we always take the way forward! And then, coached by some sea faring being, we know exactly what the storm is all about. It is meant to rip into us, and have its way with us – but not now.

Blake – Listening closely to the wind, a second form of storm – on land. This storm is meant to tear us asunder – but we understand it now, and its effects, and so we can continue on our way. But here we must be careful. Fear not, we will win!

Head in the clouds, heart in all that we do. There is a movement here of this to that, from here to there, from now to then. And in this movement is the world - the world and all she sees. Come, to the furthest landing. This is a place of acuity and of poise.

Blake – stepping away, leaning back – the hold on us is resolute. There can be no finer thing than to be at the vanguard of fate. Draw your talons, and see things that are always there. A feeling that comes, that knows its place, but goes anyway.

Almost stranger, stranger than the time piece, as it comes, and goes. The being serious for a time, and then big guffaws. Silence here, and then the room of games. Do not be perturbed, listening acclimatises.

Blake – Do you feel yourself waking? Allow yourself more time – you deserve it. Come now there is wind in these eves, we wish not to harbour spite. A mystery in the making. Having full control of our senses. We know which way to go.

A manner of speaking, that never diminishes. A heart felt dance, one that does not labour. A feeling, one that refreshes. Do not come now, but maybe later. Have a sense, a sense that rings true. Maybe in the interim, a plan, a plan of things to come.

Blake – a bland mirage, that does not contain all things. A wanting that envelopes as we see fit. What of this now, this anchor point in time? What do we see, that has not already been seen? Coming to a nice place, and never backing down.

A mild way to do things, but will it last? Do we come full sail, full circle, and full on. There is here a more desired approach. Come and be the change in the wind. Come and be that which can only go sideways, and that which always wins!

Blake - put your arm around us, and never let go. Be resilient, and sturdy, through and through. Watch as arms go by, and wink at winter. There is a time for all things. And when we see that, we know, that the larder is full, and life is for the taking.

A mist, we do not know where it came from. A laugh, from a person we can't see. And then, without thought, we climb again, for one more time, climb the aegis of the sun, from where we cannot tell, from whom we cannot say. Be true.

Blake – A constant refrain, that has no recourse to the fibre of things, but to its heart. There is like a newly won belief, in the raiment that shields from the cold and wet. What have we now, but the solemnity to continue.

A sort of rain dance that lasts a good part of the day. What we beseech of the tide is that it continues with composure, until the parting of the way. Here there will be a truce, before all things. Until that time the invective will be yours.

Blake – Now we come to the order of things. Dice are thrown, but what of the maple? There are times ahead, in fullness of girth. And here before the line in the sand is dashed by sea water, we catch a glimpse of what is to come.

William Blake

And now, what do we do, that stands the test of things. There is a place – we don't know where. There is a time - we don't know when. There is a silence, despite the temperature. And here where the news is from the outer reaches, life, and all that is.

Blake – A gate with nothing on it. A sign that calls for peace. Are you Blake, someone to consider for the times, someone with passion, and no fear of what is to come. There echoes the sentiment of the stride, to find as lingering in it.

Forgetting not how, nor why, nor what for, there is a grace that has as its spark the merriment of the wind as it dives and turns and steels us. Come now, a further turn we do not know. A further temperance we have not found. Be here – will you.

Blake, are you a friend to us, and to all? Does your bathing leave you clean enough? Are you what wishes to be clean, cleaner than the rest? Do not find yourself an aggregate, in times of straight ease. What more can we say, until the show.

Forgoing, not forsaking. Having the tangent to will our way through. What is more a stiff upper lip helps shield us from the storm. Do not be long, we cannot wait for things. And here where the nighttime is a rush, we come again, for all that is.

Blake – a crucible in the middle of it. A segway that knows no headway more than moisture can contain. There is now a newness, that does not refine. Come now, a sense we have that all will be well. There is now a path to follow.

Firsthand knowledge of what it takes. Firsthand knowledge of what it means. A truer sense of the now and the water, joined together. The fibre of things. What is more, the last point in the join is our favourite. Come now, be here.

Blake – what do you say to us, now we are here? Is this where we weep tears of gold, tears of blue. There is enough here to find the mark. And when we sing, we sing like we cannot miss a beat, and then like seashells in the daylight – we come.

The sense we have that we have already made it – and then like an all-encompassing sound, we believe once again that life can be virtuous, and in no need of help. Come now, a further rinse through the trees, and then, there.

Blake, there is time. Blake, there are things to overcome. Blake, are you there? Do we come, from here to there? Is this where we find

William Blake

ourselves, on these hills, do we have a way, to come down from the sky in unending bursts? Do not be concerned.

The foam of the top of it. The time to say goodbye. I have never really known peace here. But now I am there, where thistles do not grow. Come now, do not pulse, there is abandon here, that does not list. We have come for you, and all will be well.

Blake – does your vision pursue the font? Is this where it lies? Ear marked for destiny, and have the child arrive. Stay still I urge you. There is what has been foretold. And in the measure of it, enough to come for the revelry.

A side issue that has nothing left to give. A heart in manger that believes itself to be the one. Come now, forever in the way of it. There is a folding point we don't understand. I have given in to this force, but for too long.

Blake – are you weary of the daylight? Does your spirituality sense the dawn? Are there things here that do not fit. Do you love where you now are? Your effect has been very large. Do not squander, there is no more time. Verily and with guile.

Mismatched and able, being the one who stays the course. There is here much more to do, and much more to say. And here, where we have never missed a beat, there comes a landslide of ideas that teeters on the way of it.

Blake – do you stop and smell the roses? Are you able? Do you come for great things; things untold – this much is certain. Will the life of it change complexion upon delay? There is nothing ever remiss here. But what of the day – we will see.

Adventures in the land of mist. Where does this leave us? Somewhere special. Somewhere sharp. Somewhere unpronounceable. And here, where the sea is never laughed at, a calculable delight, that shimmies through to each portion of it.

Blake – you seem keen, you should have a go at it. And that is what he did – despite all protestations. Never minding the heat of it. The glare, the levering, and the solace. Do not be the one to care too closely for it, the instant he is there.

Addressed to you Blake! This much I know. And here, where the night is like a sort of reminiscing, there rises in the fibre of it something we have not seen before, and that is that milk and honey will sew their seeds in much the same way they always have.

William Blake

Blake – do you feel the way there? Is this the time of year? Do we fly figuratively in our dreams? And then is there more to say? More to whisper? More to hold close? Only live for it, and then, never live without it. And here, a resting point – yes.

Assignation and commitment – a sense we all have. Never believe in the trope that brought us here. There are times, and then there are times Let the weathering of the sun cast it pall. Never falling behind – only looking ahead. One two three, go!

Blake – do you feel interchangeable? Is this the way to go? Is the sound of it making you near-hearted? Are the times in need of narrowing. Do not submit the test for it, this much is clear. And then, like a tapestry of golden thread, significance!

There is a chance amongst it. There are demons within. There is sport to be had. There are things to be left behind. What of that, yes, do we say enough, or ransom our clothes like radish skin to the twilight. Nary a thing to see.

Blake – do you comprehend the night sky? Is this where we go, into neverness? Do you want the same as everybody, but your own individual desires? Come now, are you sick? Sick of the fog, and the bracing of what should be. Fortune up!

Offended, and delineated – we will come for that. And here, where sport mars the template, there is a majesty that cannot be derived for anything or anyone. Is it harder to see things as they rise, despite the resignation of the day. Yes indeed.

Blake – is the spring an officious time for you – does it drive you to things to come? Be not prouder than now. In this new formulation is that which we know should happen. Come now, do not feast yet – there are tales to tell, and folk to remember!

Take your hat off – be in tune with the day. Tread this thing called fate, and see how it rises. And then, without the slightest need, a windpipe to the sky. Causing nothing to be unhinged, we carry back and forwards all of the sum of it.

Blake – a thought for you. What is the longest time it has taken to write a book? I bet you don't know. You said your epic poems seem to have taken a labour of a long life, but did not. But how long for the longest time to write a book? A life-time?

I will break shackles here and now. And then, like a mariner out pipped and out witted, who still boxes on, finally winning his bout. There is now something to say, and I will say it – never tread on the toes of someone who is losing; pain be you.

William Blake

Blake – a thing we must not see! A traipsing that listens closely. A pile of sand that never becomes anything else. A figure of speech that has no time to reflect. What is there more than this – more than this – no nothing – verily.

Conscious of the need of things. There was once a gift, that had, as its place, all the roundness of the heart. And here, where the life of the mast is laden with sails from the east, there captures a rain that has no need to fall. Resolute.

Blake - a sense of calm that that doesn't know when to sleep. A feeling we had before the dawn. There is more time here than we could ever imagine. Let the dust settle, and what you will find will bring you down to raise you up. Yes, please.

Forthcoming, and not diving. Being in check, and then moving out. The nest is here for the taking, do not go walking without it. And here, where the soul reaches, the magnificence of the journey rides through. Come now, do not divide.

Blake – somethings remain, and somethings are lost. And then, when the hay from the fields becomes an object of art, here the feeling of camaraderie is strong. Do not merely listen to us, go and find out for yourself. This is strong. Yes.

What we say, is not something that should be said. What we do, is not something that should be done. But in the meantime, where the clouds are here in numbers, there will be a station that has no gap to fill. Come now, no applause is needed.

Blake – sailing on the wind of it. It is a wind that labours in unknown ways, in untold fashions, in numerous incarnations. Do not devise a plan here, it will not settle the matter. Be a soothsayer in a land of hills. But never come down.

Vestiges of what ignites – a chasm that isn't hollow. There and then movement, we come to the settling of the way. Do not believe entirely in what you see, there is dirt in our eyes. Do not linger in what you make of it. The town is close at hand.

Blake – do you quell that thing inside that does not agree with you? Is this the maelstrom and the vigour? Do you cope in quarters, and then in halves. Next to this is nothing, nothing of the daylight. Do we stand on toes for minutes or hours?

The wrinkling of a lassitude out of its comfort. Nearing the way in, and forgiving the way out. Here where there is nothing left to give, the newness of it all surprises. Come, and be quick, the stallion does not err. The semblance of a twilight.

Blake – There are times that do no harbour, and times that are reluctant. Have the hardship wander, and I will mention one thing more. And in this, a tempest blast that can always be resolved. What is more, the niceties of our work sing.

Having something more to chew on. Having the mast, and seeing it through. Being something more to the votive crowd! Never in our wildest dreams do we see things this straight. The sense we have that the kindness we receive is what we truly need.

Blake – does the sun blaze on you? Does the viciousness of the walk perturb you? Come now, it is all mild here. And when we have something more to hold onto, there comes a vintage nestling, one that only harbours the day.

Come now, further seeds need sewing. And here a regretful ambience permeates the square. And then, a trail of smoke from a fire that has never stopped burning. What makes it burn so? – It is the world, as it turns on winter's ease.

Blake – do not stop now, the thing that holds us is not the thing which binds us. And now restless fibres, fibres that make up the sky, and what we see there. Do not lie in wait, there can be only one thing to do. In treasures, be bold.

Withholding all approaches, we laugh at the space that is left. Come now, further near than far, we leverage the kind of life the sands want. And then, without any semblance of what we should need, a force of nature descends!

Blake – come full speed, and see the journey for what it is. Do not allay your fears, but augment them, and ride them rife. There is never enough here to fully steer the boat. But this is more than we had ever thought to be. Come now, be entrenched!

Alike in so many ways, we can never caution the asking of the price. And here where love and all her entreaties has not the strength of it, we come now to this part of the world, and know that ease is not an easy thing to acquire. Be what is said.

Blake - a thought we once had, but cannot shape. A feeling that turns on its own self. A sort of bounce that is in step with the courageous. What we thought was home, becomes a place to stay in passing. What is this thing? We do not know.

William Blake

Looking for the time of day. It seems as if the shirt is on a back of strength. And then, where the moisture of a winter's night only prolongs things, there is a listening that breaks the spell of hardship – what will come will come.

Blake – do you suddenly feel great, as if you can do anything? Is this what we have come for, something to alleviate the malady? There reaches into souls a glimpse of future bliss. There is now a solemn rite, that harks as it delineates, yes, for now.

Much like the nuance of it. What is fair, is tidiest. What is long without is here to stay. And then, a feeling that time is just here to use its wit. But that is okay, we worship at her door, like a breathtaking scene from nature. Hurry then, we will find a way.

Blake – are you sure of missing things? Does the tailor not suit? Is this what we see when we fall, and get back up again? Where is the cost of it? What is the dread we feel at the sight of it? Sense amongst the nonsense. We will see again.

The lost half. Where is it, and where did it come from? Where do we find ourselves now, without it? The drumming our ears do to hear once again. And then, a noise from above. There is here no sense to any of it. But we must try, and in trying, increase!

Blake – come and see the way of it. It is a magical thing. It starts with a hand clap, and measures itself in time beats, off the right, and then left, then up, then down. Do not envisage anything more. The sense of it is here, and we know it.

Casting through the blades, we have a new toil to undertake. There is nothing left of what we once were, and now the slate is clean, we will have some fun. Do not find ourselves amiss, the signs of it do not tread lightly. Come only when you can.

Blake – a message for you, my friend; it reads – "Do not come now, the signs of it are not positive". Do not forsake an old friend during these times. We are worthy of something else! And here, casting something more into it, is life-affirming.

A little bit of the mill in proceedings, never really hurt. But tell me now, what is it that you seek. What is it that you hang your hat on? After all of this, there comes a landing on the lake of lives, and here, where we sing that one note!

Blake – a simplicity of it that knows only the treasure of life. Do not tumble down the hill, it is too high! And then, with a trusting hand, the discomfort subsides, and what is left no longer interferes with things as they come. Do not pronounce, things will be.

All and outstanding, come for the new condition of the wreck. And here, where nothing is sung in its entirety, there is motion towards the heavens, and a sailing towards the night. Do not send me. I am here to watch. This much is clear.

Blake – do you gather up the ornamental rocks, and shield them through the garden. Is this your garden with the soldier? Excellent, you are there. I knew hope would come to you sooner than later. Never mind the stage, it is full of those things.

Above the mark. What is through is through. Now, turn this way, and see yourself in the shadow. Light comes here, from a source that is both a mystery and a fallacy. There is time enough to let the feet walk where they want. Fortuitously we are found.

Blake – holding court with best of them. You loved a good literary gathering. And then, without the briefest thought, the love of the cadence came over you, and you remembered where it all came from. This much is true, fortitude is in the mind.

Never before have we seen such adventure on the high seas. And on land to. There is a dimension to life that has as it noise barbs of winter rain. Come now, do not disguise, the light is here, and casts us forth into the day without rejoinder.

Blake – a salience that turns in untold ways. A feeling we had, and now have, that things will turn out all right. This is a mystery, and a blessing. But what of the guard? What happens to them? The feeling of this is a gauging. Not to be ratified.

Caution here. Caution there. The mistletoe does not know where to land. Come now, there is more to life than that cauldron, we must only think of what is next. Urizen, the power of your reason, checks passion and desire. Yes, and despite, we have it.

Blake – the sound it makes, hauls itself into our consciousness, like a bitter wind, that has only drawers to keep memories in. And in these places that are temperate in themselves, the boisterous and the calm never find solace to live. Be kind.

A beauty of the sea – do you come for us on land, as if by fate compelled? Is this what we see of you, most enamoured? Can we believe in things once again? Do you take your toll, and by strength of sight, capture what is around you.

William Blake

Blake – do you seem to float, away from the basket of things? Is this where we have come to? The hardship of the mountain side is never too gradient. Come to feel what is next! Come and be a gradient by the shore. It could suffice.

A neatly shaped ornament that carries an inscription – come and be privy to life to all she bends. And then something more – come to the show of life. And that was it beauty in its element. Do not curtail the language, it deserves to be said.

Blake – a coastline that reverberates through time. A sense we have that the twilight is here for what comes next. I have no smaller thought than this, and that is – whispers are here for us. Do not depend on any other thing.

A wishing well, that uncorks the bottle. A listening that deserves nothing less. And then, as if by magic, we are in that place, one we have not been to in a long while. Creeping into line, we see ourselves in motion for the lasting of things.

Blake – hiding inside the house, only coming out for a glimpse of things to come. It is here that we chase for further things. Be the motion of the stars, there is nothing like it. And here, where motion is not of a type, we come, for the solidity.

Forging ahead, trying not to fall. And here, where we walk with longer strides, there is no need to take our time. And then, despite what we have seen, a lasting feather, as it floats once more towards the earth. Do not dull your senses, come.

Blake – a force of nature, this feeling of ours. We sense that nothing more will do. And here, where the landscape is nothing other than a rarefied mixture of air and water, a stream of life, as it overcomes many obstacles. Now we care.

Quite simply, spectres in the wood. And then, without the nourishment to continue, we service our carriage, and know the journey to be rough. Sitting back, we have only one concern, and that is heart – where will the heart take us? Yes, a concern.

Blake – have you seen the wood? The place of exteriors, where the plant life flourishes, the trees inaugurate, and the wildlife does something special. And here, where the daisy and the thistle believe in something new, a respite, to freshen.

Happening despite our leaves of joy, there inculcates a new lesson of life. Do not follow the wanderer, he lives in times of ease. Only follow those who have been to the labyrinth. And then, to see things again, we open our eyes, and there we have it.

Blake – a tendency to dream for long periods. Does this seem propitious? I believe it must. There are times that do not stay the course. Here are some of them - Cyclical, harassed, inculcated. And then, despite it all, a victory for the ages.

Nearing things as they happen, we send our lullabies through to different times and places. It is here we push forward to new destinations, and new climes. Do not bend the vicissitudes – we need them. So come closer, we will see what we can see.

Blake – sensing the reverse of it all, we plunge into harbour hearts. Sing no more, there is not time. Be not one to echo on shores of the departed. There is here a fundamental sweep, that tailors in, and tailors with. We will not at first sight fall!

Gaining in stature, the hearth we find does not collect wood. And in the meantime, where the tenseness of the round fills us with strength, there has with us someone to go to, if only for a short while. I will not think too soon. To do so is in error.

Blake – have the rain stop at a thought. Have the closing of speed know what is next to next. The forming of undeniable rifts, that come back on themselves in times of pleasure. And then, without a single care, the well-spring transfigures the night.

Never care for what was. It is what is now that pertains. Pertains to the wellbeing of the plaintive melody. Do what you say, and do it well. There are never things to deride on, never one single thing. And now there comes to pass a future we all want.

Blake – do you come in times of trouble, or times of ease? This much beckons as it calls, a withering, and a substance to it all. I will not find us ready. Ready for the uptake of tradition anew. Do not labour the way we all do, in these motions.

At the heart of it, we see ourselves, now more than ever. Come now, a sensing of the time of day. A feeling like we never were. And like something not of this world, a tension that derives itself from all that is. We will find ourselves in it.

Blake – hurtling through the wind of it, we come to a place of lost derivatives, and know that things are up in the air. But what of the sound of it? There is nothing left here. What is it that we tell of, tell our children of – everything!

William Blake

The tempting thing, is to let the snow fall where it will. And in this way, we harness all we need. Be careful not to shout, and unnerve the life of these trees. There is now something more to delineate. Something to shield us, running still.

Blake – do you see all you need to see? Is this what is left of us? To placate the sands, as they move in time to the ballast and the repartee. Come now, nothing moves as fast as this. Come and be a tribute to the lines of this motion.

A grating sound, from where? Do we hear ourselves in this, as a sun tells the time? There is here something misplaced, as we never knew it to be. And then, to march again through the distance, and the temptation to feel itself go.

Blake – do you love what is here? And then, like a passing remembrance, a piece of good fortune rears up, and says in a bold voice, 'yes we are with you, there is time to make you new.' Come now, the scene loses itself in the well.

Good and solid – it will stand the test. And here, where the lake is not one to tarry, the morning mist rears like it was holding something of value. Be interested in the dawn, much comes from this. And now, hear us all, as we work and rest.

Blake – a strong beginning, how do we finish? –
With the strength of an ox. Do not be one to
abandon us, we are here for you. And then, like a
sea wave that has not found itself yet, we rally for
the time being, and see ourselves simply here.

Graining in the midst of it. We know what it is to
finish something. There is a chance to come, that
when we are there, and the firelights are through,
there will be an apprentice, much like yourself,
Blake, who will guide us to our chosen vantage.

Blake – come inside, my dear man. Do not be the
one to fold up in this heat. Come and find your
way like the rest of us. And here, without the
slightest hesitation he does. And that was that. But
what of the churning on the hillside? Enough!

Converging, and thrilling. Surrendering to the
night. There is more to this heartbreak than the
well-spring ever dreamed. And then, like a fireside
poem, the dreamiest depths of a thousand ruined
castles come to be true! We must continue.

Blake – do you see yourself now? Do you see
yourself as you want to be. Your fire, is our
delight. And then, casting forth to level out, we
managed to rumble together a fire of our own. But
what is it? How is it made? We will see shortly.

William Blake

This is how it goes – forwards and then backwards, up, and then down! Round and then through. There is nothing left of us after this. But what we do know, is that the sealing of wax on the envelope is enough to bend the light, and then, well see!

Blake, come now, do not be reminiscent of the storm. There is always a way through. We have not seen things here lightly, nor have we dreamed that each of us has a story to tell. And then, without fanfare nor delight, we use our strength anew.

A homegrown running, does not entail the way to go. And here, where the firelight is enough to dismiss our demons, we live in the moment, and see what is next. We will not linger on the shore, nor yell at the sea. There is more than enough time to see.

Blake – do the words mean anything to you – they do! Music! And here where the sense we have of foreboding is vanquished upon the stroke of nine, there is a lot to say. But what of us now, now that time has stopped. We will find a way!

In amongst it – fighting through. Having not the need, and still relishing. The simplicity of it all.

Now and again. We close our eyes, and never see a thing. The tempest is quick, but we have the tenacity to overcome.

Blake – letting ourselves be, and then walking up those hills. Do we see things now, that keep us in line to the treasure of the afternoon. What keeps us here is not what we say, but what we do. Be the departed, but as they come back.

The forward motion of it all. Wrangling past, and through. I will not see aspects of it, until the end. And here, without steps, nor singing, we come to that place that has the time it takes, the time it takes to settle the wheel – so there you go.

Blake – a sense we have that the tried and true is enough. The lighting is new, but what of it? There is a likeness to the few and to the many. Come to the cause of it, there will be time. There is much to be said, and much unsaid.

There is a place, within every beating heart. There is a window, that looks onto every sea. And here, where the night is not so long, and the daylight hours never diminish, something more than what trundles embarks, then is away.

Blake – a ritualistic display, that harbours the rings around our fingers. There is never the slightest inclination, to be this, or otherwise. The temptation is there, to exude the whispers of fate, and all that she will continue with.

Holding out for the sun. We beach ourselves in front of the sign, and simply read all we can. There is nothing more to do here, all is in readiness. But wait, what is this? Is this what we have been waiting for? A new tide that reigns in the old.

Blake - What is wrong with this picture? Something to do in the way of it. There is something we do every day, that is not represented here. But what is that? – we will let you decide! Come now, and away with all that is. Do not listen for the middle of it.

Foreign to our shores, there is more than a mindful entreaty, one that labours on in the most tremendous ways. The silence we hear is nothing more than beauty itself. And here where the arches of indifference beckon, we see ourselves fully.

Blake – are you the one to contend, for that round up of writers? Is this what it takes to rouse your interest? I hope you are coming to the ball? It will be nice to see you! Never wander further, further than you have ever done before.

A listing of the ship, that sails till noon. There is something here, that we never thought would delay us. And that is nothing, nothing in the way. Come and be placated, there is much time. And so it is, until the round ends.

Blake – come to our endeavour. See what you think, and try the proximity to the harbour. There is beauty that lurks here – but not for too long at least. Conditions that do not appal, at least we don't think so! Come with us now, we will surprise.

A fawning through the day, never enough to say. Come now, a lot of the features of this house are there in this one! But what of it – shall we dance the merriment of old, or the merriment of new? There is a lot to stumble through. Let us embark.

Blake – a nice thing to settle on. But what of the of the feel of it. There are here things that fit, and things that don't. Let us be the difference in the weather, sometimes here, sometimes there, sometimes roundabout.

The personal sphere. And here, where we succumb to so much, there is a longing to be near, and not far – a longing to be here and not there – a speaking to be close and not harangued. Do be the sound of things, it will count for so much.

William Blake

Blake – do you have more of yourself than ever before? Is this what you say you will do, and often don't? Come in close, there is a need to talk. But what of the harrowing? A new need to fight the bannisters? What of it all? We will come.

Arching like the seasons, but never tempted to right ourselves. There is a time linked to this, that asks of itself, why this? And here, where we have not the thought to run a mile, there belongs a fibre of the soul that exhales anew. Be firm, things will settle.

Blake – come my good man, there are things in neither heaven nor earth that compare to this. What is it now, that we have thrown down the glove? What is it now that the times wish to envelop?

Advancing beyond measure. There lies a keepsake, that turns on no road. Be a little surprised, there can only sense a new path. And then lost in the chase. There are paths we wish never to go down. But what is this – something else?

Blake – do you sit on cards? – is this where we rush? In this instance, the rough has way of the sport. And here, where the town is in close proximity to the road, we see ourselves again, walking down, and around and through. But where are we now?

A simpleness, that sees itself through. A many-sided object, that believes in itself. Never once landing awkwardly. A chance to quell the viciousness of it all. Do not stand, but run. But ease into it, there are things to do – we must not be late. Yes.

Blake – is this the sort of thing we mean? Is this the sort of tenacious belief we all have? And here, where the furthest sight cannot see, there lies an ancient pasture, one that goes with the flow of it. And now, a new sense to believe.

Developed in years, time has been kind you. And then, with a like-minded attention to the cusp, there sings an apogee to the ground. Do not be a fool for it, once should be plentiful. There is now a strong renown for all that is found.

Blake – like all that is missed, the feeling we have is like a lake - a lake that has nothing to be squared. But in turns, the motion of it stirs a quiet silk. Do we find ourselves rushing despite? Do we find the way through and beyond?

All in the midst of the semblance of things. The matter is not here, as it is not there. Consider the task at hand one of adventure. And here, where night-time has its sway, the desperation of one soul to another does not suffice. Here we must linger.

Blake – a sort of standing, that registers the age, has come to be, and not be – further now than ever, we sing for our supper. There is only one chance at redemption, and this is it. Only on chance, and then we are there.

Clinging onto things, for life and leisure. Being like a subsisting thing, without the need. There is a likeness to the sea, but with only what comes close. A sense we believe in things, surer than the tide. A broadside that festers no wound.

Blake – When you returned to London after your trial, Catherine developed a rheumatoid condition, probably as a result of the case. She recovered, and all was well. And then onwards for you, and through. Much like things – brimming.

A sound that does not escape. A feeling we once had, but have now forgotten. There are lights here, candles that close no aplomb. And then, with a heady stare, there comes a ghost to tread down the ages. Do not believe in him, he only comes.

Blake – a nestling in close. And now, fireflies
diminish our sense of return. Come now, things
only wait for us to return in small numbers.
Wishing for the dawn, we hardly see ourselves at
all. What we do see, is nothing other than a lake in
the sun.

Moisture, and a certain bringing. There is life,
where there was once death. And here, where the
fearsome and the jovial renounce in good time,
there sits a new tree to renounce the old. Come
now sisters, do not see the climbing as a hardship.

Blake – what is this for, this continual motion? Do
we have as out of the centre the mist of a
thousand mornings? Is this what earth is for? And
then a merriment to rival all souls. There has been
a rupturing in the way. No longer, it has passed.
Yes.

The spring is here, but what of the harp. The birds
do not fly to their own dimensions. Only in and out
of love. In love – out of love, like all things. And
then a silence to rival all silences – and then, a
sort of whistling that has as its heart the wall of
desire.

Blake – standing on a hill, leaning forwards –
having the need to hold on, and never let go.
Desperation and condolences. Whisperings and

the fate of all things. Can we say more than we
are told? This much will last – this much will stay.

Confusion in the ranks, handywork in the dream of
it. There is now a quality to it, that does not shift.
Bend your arm, and the air will support you. Be in
time, or rather, be in the times, and they will stand
by you as dirt on a windmill.

Blake – there are now a multitude of answers to
things unsaid. Never before has the nest been so
covered in the vine. There is a protection here to.
And then, without the kind of care that tempest's
dream, there comes something more. We must
see it.

Ice and water – stillness and motion. Conquest,
and delivery, what is more. There comes a new
sense of what is right, and then, what has sight.
Do not stand in front of the line, it is a divide of all
things. And now, despite, a whistling to guard.

Blake – gathering rose petals by the forest's edge.
Can we ever have our fill. We see ourselves more
this time than ever has been seen. There can be
nothing more than this. Nothing more than a
Sunday retreating from the world.

A hill in favour – in favour of so much. There is
here a motion than cannot be scrapped, for

anyone, or anything. Don't see yourself as in the distance, see yourself up close, and then when the motion of the stars grabs hold, jubilation.

Blake – a sort of whirring sound that captures what we have and sends us once again into the deep beyond. The same sound catches us and brings us back, in such amazingly good form, that we don't know what to do with ourselves

Conscious of the art of it, we see ourselves rushing through the world, in times undeniable. And there, where we are most at home, a dreaming that lasts a second, has the means of us all dreaming to a minute. This much can never be told.

Blake – consider yourself a man among strangers. There is here a haven for your regret, and a solace for your soul. Are you pleasantly surprised? Come now, things are here from the transcribing, and we will take nothing more than a second look.

A feeling like the cobwebs have been dusted. And here, where the solemn and the true combine in ancient ways, there belongs a new need to watch, and watch go. Come now, the further we search, the further we belong.

William Blake

Blake – do we know which way we are going? Which way forward, which way back? There pronounces the fjord, and what do we say to that? There is an ancient track that knows which way to go, and pushes you in that direction. Yes, helpful.

A state unknown, and undelivered. What have we commenced but all that is? What have we thought but all that can be? I have known something special, but have not forgotten its dimensions. There are things that do not pace, and things that do.

Blake - will you come with me? To petition what we see as ours, to return the wandering of what is left? And then, without thought nor care, an arrival to be summoned on magic chairs and magic tables. We will win, everyone.

A union, that is written in the stars. And here, given the heart of it, we see our names in solemn walk. A walk that destinies claim. And here, despite ourselves, we run for cover, and ourselves full of heart. We will come here, and know ourselves true.

Blake – a feeling we thought we had lost, has returned. And here, despite the collateral, there is a new voice to be heard. We have launched our ships here, and know them to be safe. A sense we had, that the masts were tall. Yes.

Something unhinged, is not the tempest itself, but the blame we place at the feet of us all. Somehow we continue, and find ourself with small naps, and then, a belief that things are strong, and will not stop. Come now, all that is and that will be.

Blake – what of your deliverance, to the voice of which you do not become. Hope, and a treat – a treat of well-spring water – and the respite of an age. Never before have we seen this – never before have the rounds been so precise.

Be prefigured in all you do. Be the chalice, and the temptation will be gone. There is now much to be said, and much to be done. Never let the finders stay on board. There is more than is here. The sound in the attic is especially lucid.

Blake – do you see yourself in full regalia – the university of life. I hope this hasn't cheapened things for you. And now, with a splash of water, hearts are set on blaze - is this what we have come for? I believe so. And then a chance at it!

Mysteries, and vials of the unknown. There are now times in between times that do not live, and only skerrick through in unison. I will never give a moment of this. Wish us a soft landing. Come now, farrows are hardy, and never found.

Blake – a feather in the midst of it. What we thought was a danger, was nothing other than a solace - come now, hold on to what is, and what will be will surely follow. There is something more to answer. We will guide.

A little bit of tension to the fire in our eyes. Come now, sport is here for laughter. Yes now, a belief in awe of it. There comes a magnificence in the way of it. We shall not time. And here much that is fresh, and in abundance.

Blake - have the stalls your name on them? Is this what it takes? Is this what we must do, do to placate the crowd? I think I have it, and I think I can revel in its wears. There is something we must only do on occasion – and that is think, think deeply.

Advanced, and yet slow. Needing to move, but purely ensconced. There was a time, where we stood shoulder, to shoulder. There was a time when things basked in dreaming. And here, where the tenacity of the night itself dreams, much more to say.

Blake – holding on, never sure, always pertaining, but not for a window view. There are times in amongst it when the living, and the idle, take sway, and what is left is enough to hound the entrenched for a day. Believe in what you like.

Never enough to truly say. And then, a masquerade of it, to send ourselves flying. And now, for the round-a-bout way of saying things. We live, in toil, and we breathe in sweat. There is a time for change, and more than a wisp of longing to suit the day.

Blake – we know what is left. We know how the seeds of a larger turning confound us. And here, where the word is spoken, spoken in the much-maligned streets, there rings a bell to be true by. And now, without thought – exuberance, and place.

Something like the last of it – something like the first of it – something like this. We halt, and know our place. We halt, and let our place be known. Come now, do not speculate, there is more to envisage. And here, a challenge for the rest of us.

Blake – do you stay, or do you go? Is this what the journey brings? We have an incision to make. To where all dreams are kept. And what we will find will shock a nation, and rule the day in times of utmost joy. Utmost!

William Blake

Never considering things worthy, never being sure of the plenitude of the night. There is time – there is always time. And here, where the signage never beckons, a token to be reckoned with. Here, I say, here, never stand in the way.

Blake – do you wonder still – wonder at the things to come? This much we have been given, but what of the acceptance, and the tail of twilight guesses? There is a catching of winter sun that transpires the untold in us all.

Folding in trays of afternoon delight, there comes a fathoming that only heralds what is there anon. We never thought to speak this way about anything or anyone. But when we get down to it, the mischief of the daylight has as its cousin the first chief.

Blake – when back in London you were commissioned of the Blair project – Blair's The Grave. And here where life seemed in tune, you came to life with a new found sense of application. What is more you knew your worth.

Afternoon, in the garden - so pleasant and so delightful. What have we felt will be here for a further year. Come now, do not renege, do not say there is no point to it. There is a folly of reminiscence here. Do something well, and we will see.

Blake – are you strong, do you galvanise at key times? There can only be a heart here, a heart to hear with. What is this thing called love? What is this thing called a stage? We have come to take charge, and then, take a second look.

There is a sense we have to weave our nest, in time to a song about a day. Do not belong, it is like a swift attack, that harbours the prescient and the domed. What is this we feel? What is this that comes along?

Blake – do you harbour winter crews? Is this what we say to the steepness and the fall? There is like the edge of the rainbow, as she comes walking all the while. What do they say? What do they say, and then give directions for the road ahead?

A belonging, that starts its life, so infinitesimally small, that to grow is to set it on the trail to the beyond and back. And here, where tiny movements absolve all doubt, there is a chance at something special. Do not release the sky, but give respite.

Blake – are you the one to believe in things still? Is this what you do, evoke the half-rite to fuel a passion? You are there my friend, we must not tarry. Delectable and delightful, we see ourselves thriving, and here a moisture to rinse with.

A sense of friendship. A sense of what has preceded. A sense of the distance between two points, and what can be achieved therein. There is a space, a great space, that opens as between two lovers – a space that knows and breathes.

Blake - and then, with the makeshift rattling, there comes a feeling that harbours all we know. Blake, do you come encumbered, like the sky in its splendour? There are now things that do not hurt, and that give way to light.

Climbing up that hill, we see ourselves in wonder and in silk. Hanging on for pure fun. We love what we have, and love what we do, so here we say – do not linger, there will be time ahead. Blisters on the knees of it. Convivial things.

Blake – are you encased in mystery? Is this what we do to fathom our depths? Do you know which way you wish to go? Is this something you should know? Is this something that a bashful sorrow should feel in touch with?

A sort of attachment to the water! Is this how we feel things are? Stopped, and invigorated. Clover and deliverables. That much is in us, and through

us. Come now, there is time as there is always a
way. Never mind the effect, there is a way.

Blake – do you hear the hush of tones? Is this
where we shall find you? Up against it, and
through the while? This much is said, that when
we are gathered, a false roof engenders the
scene. Rock on rock, on fleece on cajoling whip!

A little bit of light work to envelop what is left. Can
we say, simply, that there is nothing to keep us
motionless. And here, where tears have been
shed, there is a light that burns, burns in deepest
yellow. Come now, a sense of the new to keep us.

Blake – is this what we find when we look? Is this
what we have when we find? Condolences Blake,
you are left to unhinge the plaything. And there,
with gossip abound, a place of difference across
from the well. How is the water?

Considering what we have left, we are in a good
position. There are bits of this, bits of that, pieces
of this, pieces of that. And when the cauldron runs
hot, there is just nowhere else to go. So we sit,
and wait, and speak of what is sure.

Blake – envisioning the tempest and the blast.
Imagining the harvest, there is something like
minded about all of this. But here, we are staunch,

and we do not relinquish to the night. But what have we left, except all that is? We will come.

A therein lies the truth of it. Therein lies what can be ascertained. It is a piece of innocence we lost as a child, but now have the steam to gather once again. Something great lies here. Something that only has half of life – but all of it to build.

Blake - seeing the untold, feeling what is left. There is much that labours in the way of it. There is much that labours away from it. And here, where we see ourselves with fresh eyes, we notice our good looks have returned! For now!

Considering things at their core, there are many traipsings that we must review. And here, where the noise of days is not something we must endure. There is now a temporal stance that sings its tune to nobody but the heart of things. Yes a start.

Blake - full to the brim, and not knowing what to do. Full to the brim, and only vying for what comes next. There is a chance here, a chance at something new. What have we found ourselves but a trail through the mist. Here we will be.

Furthermore, the time it takes to harvest a field is that which also it takes to fathom a question, and then its answer. And yes, there is a languishing that bears no fruit. But what of the sound of it, time knows no wounds? Come and be fond.

Blake – a courting of the rest of it. A courting of the field. A courting of the red of it. There is not something here we should try. But only let come at intervals of nine. And this will keep us coming up through the temperate regions, for a spell at least.

Not knowing which way to go, the wrestling of the truce is enough to placate us. Much which is not done, can remain so, and much which is done, can also remain so. And here, where the great gradient is not what it seems, much foraging to do.

Blake – hosting the reverie to its natural resting point. There is a sense we can make it. There is a sense we can truly be. There is a plateau, one upon which we sit. And here, where pain is furthest from us, we sit and talk, and even enjoy our lives.

Trusted figures of times equipped. Trusted figures of down to effort bowls, that have sense instead of nonsense. Leap forwards, and not backwards. Leap away, and not through. Have this as a causeway, it will suffice. Come now, let us be congenial.

William Blake

Blake – a touch, and then forever. A silence, and then the stars align. What is left of things in the water, as we trace ourselves again in sand? What is left of things in the water, as we trace the mysteries of this life in bubbling brooks?

What is there left? What is left of the night? Can we challenge ourselves to a duel, and be prepared to wait? Can we be the things that meander, but hold on to chosen time? There is like something before all this. We will wait and see.

Blake – a homespun riddle. Something like the last of it, near the shore, near the waves, near where it becomes sentient. And then as we speak of things that forage, a new incentive to burrow. There is a face beyond all things.

Next to things which creep. Next to things which seep. Next to things which say, hey hey. A lot falls on the backs of what are now lines in the sand. And here, where we know ourselves to be full of strength, and full of life.

Blake – in recovery from the world. In hope that the changes will remain. In hope that the decisions made here will only linger in time to the seas rally. And when, we immerse ourselves in wonder, there is never more time to see things through.

What makes it a time of it? What makes us see things straight? In the middle of this hill, we stand upright, and see the dutiful and the bold strain through. And then, a herald to the call aloud – one we see not as our own temperament. Lest we survive.

Blake – a heart that beats with red exchange, is nothing other than the desperation of the eye-line foraging for a true embrace. Do not remain for a moment longer, the time has now passed, and lifts things higher.

Abysses, and those absolved. Those absolved, and those decried. What we have here, is something greater, greater than the talents of a thousand players, all hitched in one. Greater than you and me, and the ladder of fate. We see again. Thankyou.

Blake - a simple display of the grandiloquent, to put you off what you are eating. As we form short-term displays of our own. And then a missive that comes addressed to you. Imagine that! Now! And here we have something more to say!

And then, around the middle of it all, a certain source point – a heart in the world. Never denied, only to be taken as ordeal, not as find. And then, an arch above the triangles, more for us to see.

More for us to move. And then, a yell, and we have it.

Blake, do you find rhythm in life? Is this what you are looking for, even now? I hope you are ready to swim, the tempest comes, and we're shy of our boat's requirements. Do not see the foundry from here? Is this where we are from?

Commiserating, through our combined dreaming. Being blessed, and cursed and everything in-between. Be within reach of the fairy-tale, it will help, no end. And here, the tide is in definite motion. And when we encounter something sinister - laugh!

Blake – are their things to witness out here beyond the deck? Is this where we look, and through? Is this what is in the interim, supported by the indeterminable and the strained? We are here for you, and all you stand for. Come and play.

Believing in the utmost hospitality of it all. And when the glasses are half full, and turn on the reading that labels itself a fondness for the times. Chasing everything we hold dear. We are left with all of it again. Not shedding a twilight sphere.

Blake – do you find yourself swept away by the breeze of it, and not left to flee from its grasp? Do you find yourself appeased by people not of your name? And here, despite the bridge of things, much have we seen, and much have we heard!

A belief to the back and front again! Where do we love the most – or rather, where do you love the most? There can only spell derision in this space! And here we have seen nothing more than stardust in amongst it! Never give in.

Blake – half an hour, to an hour, is all I have. And here, as if by magic, the troupes arrive, and what's more they are laden. Laden with gifts from a place unknown! What do we say is our way through here? Like mist in the morning!

Conscious of the need to drive the cart home, there is left here something more ready that the seam of things. What have we seen here, other than what is. Other than what will be. Other than what cannot be driven by any horse.

Blake – like a song for the ages, like gold leaf to adorn your books. Like something special in the interim. Like a bushel in the wind that harbours fast and true. What we have here is a nestling amongst it we have not seen in a thousand years!

William Blake

Comic, and derisive -we need serious and true.
What believes itself to be ten and ferocious is not
the sound we hear from. We have seen, from this
point all we need to, and the rambunctious despite
it all. This is now your life!

Blake – atoned for the winter – the long winter.
Atoned for the chairs that sit in sequence, never
known to move. Atoned for the window, and sill,
that charters new rain, with old. What is there
here, but everything. Everything we had thought.

Antiquarian, and in demand. Seeing the quatrains,
and believing in them. Seeing what is best, and
attending to it. There comes a strategy in the blink
of an eye that sums up the situation, and resolves.
Be attentive to the wish bark – it feels.

Blake – how can we see in the distance, when to
see this far never relays the tremendous officiating
of the thing. Come and see which way to turn.
Come and see the moisture in the eve of the night
– for it is here we turn, turn for good.

Being ready, ready to situate what we find – find in
amongst the mass of things to take with us. Never
come to these cross-ways with a turn of speed,
quietly quietly, gently gently. And here there is a
now to think of. We will think.

Blake – launching forward, we see how we can
go. I am one to see things straight, not to talk in
circles, or roundabouts. And here, where we love
to roam, a feather in the trees! A feather that does
not dissipate. Be firm, and catch your breath.

Mysterious and alive, whether by chance or by
grace – it is all the same. Come to see the daylight
as a friend, not an enemy. Come and see the
torchlight as it sings, and is vociferous. Just be –
be pleased that it all has arrived!

Blake – the tentative steps of the fledgling, as she
yields no ground. The bold steps of the mother,
who will not give in. The father and his watchful
gaze. There is something primeval about this
scene, that shakes us. We will imagine!

Hovering above, the fledgling no longer is young.
She has her own family, and scurries to find some
food for her youngest. And here, without the need
to cry nor relax, a furthering of sorts toward the
aether of things. Watch here!

Blake – seething through things like something
with half-a-life. We sit, in the knowledge that
bridges will carry us all the way. What is more,
there comes a station in the park, one that needs
no hope. A flurry of activity – we have seen it.

William Blake

Verging on the sustained, we have as our motion all that is. And here, where we see better than before, a new state arises, to vet the powers that be. Come now, oceans are for thriving. Positions are made for vast aware. There is time.

Blake – do you climb back on the seat of it? Is this where the harm lays? Do you see yourself in straights, of the visionary inclusion? Can we believe what is, and what is only? Never to darken our blinds to the world! Yes, we can make it.

Forests that quarry might, and insist on being in the museum. Belief and the charge of all the horses. Sometimes we do just the right thing, and then there are times when it rains, and doesn't stop (for a while). Much a fuss made of things.

Blake – come for me, and let it be (soon). Much is thought of through the wind, and out into the day – the day of fairness of rebuke. Never once have we found things without difficulty. But that is more than we can swallow. Hold on, there is time.

A gap in the world – maybe here it will lay. Fortunate, strong and brave. I am talking to you, Blake! And then the circumstances deliver a new found sting – one that we can easily amend. What is here is never like before. We will march, upon.

Blake – has this gotten you going – the tete-a-tete of fate, and all that can be. Do not linger by the Grave, as it were. Your life is beyond, even now. Even now, that we can only see things in increments, and life. What is more, we will stand the test. Yes!

Have the strength - have the strength to see you through. Have the tenacity not to give in. Have what is here before us. There is a tempest for every one of us. Each person, a tempest. And here, there is something great. Take hold, it will come.

Blake – come to this point, and dream the dream of ages. Come to this point, and have the wish reminded. Have the stone in-between, and yours will be a mighty semblance. Come now, have as the store the fabric of things.

Have a certain reminder, that the tempest is here for a reason. Have the closing of a foe, as not just a semantic victory, but one of reality. There comes a distance that every lover dreads. There envelopes the seeds of a larger turning. Yes, and then?

Blake – have come you? Do you commission the way forward? Is this where we stand? On rocks and bounds of rocks. And here, where the silence

is not known, we come once again to all that is,
and all that will be. Be skilled, it will help.

A mis-match of colours, that had us once, but not
again. Be like the lark, heavy, and yet jovial. There
feels away, and through, and beyond, something
that harvests the rain – harvests the beating of our
hearts through and through.

Blake – do you see yourself living for a time
amongst the thistle of life? Do you see yourself
living amongst brightness of life? I would hope so.
And here, where times are spent in joy and
release, a temptation to run to the further shore.

A little-known piece of life, where the song is sung
in harmony with the many. And here, where the
temptation is to rise again, through thick and thin,
we find a semblance of things to come. But wait,
no, ask the journey. It will placate.

 Blake – cautious, yet true. Having the invigoration
to remain so. And here, where the snow never
stops falling, we find beauty through the sky, and
on the horizon. Never miss the twilight, is my
advice to you. Come, we must always visit
something again.

Gathering like rose petals on the floor. Gathering
like veracity itself. Gathering as if by the dawn.

And here, the plaintive melody of the stars rings a bow through the sky. There is now a time we can acquiesce, and find ourselves anew.

Blake – handling midnight like a rainbow. Seeing things much more quickly. Being astute to what lies before us. And now, a hard line to cross. It is here, we say hello to the resting point, and now, hello to a new point of belief.

Further reaching – but reaching for what? Further seeing, but looking for what? A taller part of you than you. A certain height amongst the trees. A certain way to go. And here, where the moisture from the leaves of the great forest amounts, we come.

Blake – having said so, we retreated, back towards the surging sea. But once there, we knew we could go forward again, and up we ran, towards our initial destination. And once here, we rejoiced, and knew the place for the first time.

A lack of memory holds us all in check. A lack of desire only holds us for a while. But here, where the sweeping of the times, has as its temperance the gold of life, there resolves a harbour to the people. Never once stray. We can bear it.

William Blake

Blake – foolishly, the world knew of what would come. But what is this, that has more than the heart to guide it? What is this, that has the wellspring, in the way of it. Come now, a further insight, one that grows with age, and height.

A festival of stars. Organising for the play. Come now, there is more to say – more to do – more to take hold of. And here, where the salt and tears of an age never know themselves to be the ship as we find it. What is this we see? Something more.

Blake – is this what we now have? Is this what we now desire? Is this what is fresh, and untimely, and with petals of chance, and of song? We listen for the cradle, and have more time for the rest. Be indeterminant with us, and there will be beauty to it.

 Forgoing, and not foreseeing. There is here a place of deep regret. There is a newness to the leaves of it, that keeps us going. And here, where the sandpipers play, there must only be a visage of it, something we can write a poem about.

Blake – are you tending to your flock, Blake? Is this your course now that you are there. Do not send us something new. Only what has been to the mill and back, as it were. And then, despite our phrasing, we love for something in the way!

A time for the rest of it – A time for the road to be re-positioned. There is no time for failure. No time for the exactness of things – yes, well maybe so. Come on friends, take a bath with it, there is no time. But we have more time than we imagined!

Blake – a curdle that rings in close. And here, we say to you, do not forge a new breath, only when the sun pieces the sky can you relax. And here, where the folly and path never mix, there comes a being of staunch regard. Yes.

Having the sense to work it out. Being one to see things through. Having the sense to it, to simply be. And then, without much more than a candle to us, we sense the time is here. But what more has fate in store for us? We will see in good time.

Blake – a journeyman, that has no fear. A journeyman that says unto the sky, 'Be what is required, and I will follow'. Be the jest in the weave of it. Be what may, and the stars will align. Come again, and wheels will guide you.

Allowed to walk, allowed to stride – permissive of the way to go. What is more than that which we have at heart. What is more than that which we have in the spring. Do not budge a muscle, there are things here that play.

William Blake

Blake – be brief, and be sensical. What have we
here, other than the lost and the found? Is this
more to us than we think? A touch stone to our
heart, a feeling to the way of it. Do not be the one
who binds, there is a cost

Galvanising, and seeing the place we arrive at.
And here, where the peace unfolds in blue
coloured paint, a sense that what we need to keep
going. And in this sense is all, and in this sense is
everything. We will only harvest what we need.

Blake – startling, and alive. Startling and remiss.
Startling to say the least. Startling in efficiency.
And then, most sought after delay in the weave of
it. Come for the collegial spirit, and stay for the
sprites. There is more to ask for than ever.

City of dust, that winds itself through the marshes,
and then along the crust of another lazing day. We
must face our fears. We must come to our play
with a sense of camaraderie, or we have nothing
left. Never be surer.

Blake – the stakes are high, but what is higher is
our hearts. We have only one, so this is what we
have in line of. Be the one to save this, and all will
be yours. Is this what we have to tailor with? That
is good, the buoyancy rattles.

Assignments, and thoroughfare. Being found to see where others can't. And now, what is left, is something of a profound location. One that harbours the deepest feelings of the species. Do not hesitate, these feelings are ours.

Blake – forthwith and intrigued. Never known despite itself. Never known, and in the way of. This is where we run to, this is where we hide. A considerable expunging of water where things reside. Never catch the way of it, chasing the moon.

Forests, and the tail of summer. Or rather, the tail of winter. And then despite myself and my deportment, there are things to do and not do. And here, where the sun languishes to the point of disregard, there are places not to see within.

Blake - Have we turned the corner? Have we seen what is next? This much is clear to us – the further reaches of the abiding is enough to fill our bucket to the brim. What is more, is that the test which stills us, is the same as the one that moves us.

Being content with things (finally), we saddle up our horse, and know that the past is the past. But then a thought, we have been like this for so long now, we will probably pass into the wind again at any moment. Let us dance.

William Blake

Blake – consummate, and at ease, we find the trail half run. And here, where the stage is set, a simple ambiance, fills it, such that we may never recover. But wait, what is this – a chance we will live at it.

Arabesque and balanced. Singing beneath the key. Never once adjacent to the time. Having more to do. Having less to be involved in. A sense we have that life remains. Being one to be sturdy. Being one to be free.

 Blake – heya hey! Here we are, again, you and I. Like bliss in a pea-pod. And then, from nowhere, a sense of what's to come. We inch forward, and tell ourselves that everything will be alright – which it will. Come now, don't despoil the scene. Yes.

And now, without a further thought, a magic trick, one the harbours all we know, and all that will be. This life upholds to virtue strong, and here in amongst we fight our fight, and know ourselves to be true. Come now, what the life will give us.

Blake – what do we say, when words are our chosen vehicle? What do we do, now that the sounds of life tarry forward, and what is next is yet to come? What do we think, when thought is all we have? We will come to some agreement. Yes.

Nestled in deep. A harrowing summer plight,
made bright, by wings on the breeze. Do we not
come in December, vowing for recompense.
There is now a fixture on the plains, that has as its
demure a tenderness that knows all.

Blake – in times of trouble, nothing more. In times
of difficulty, nothing more. And here where sport is
the plaything of the ages, there is a need to be
sharp, and square, and everything in-between.
Washing over us.

Forests that linger. A sea that has nothing left. But
what of life? It is here for the harvest. But how do
we continue? We just do, and then find a way. We
find a way through. Nectar on the cup, where it
should be. Nectar to drink.

Blake – coming forward to see more. Walking
backwards to be sharper. Closer in the feel of it,
closer that we ever thought possible. There is
much to be said, and much unsaid. There is a
tension in place, that keeps people ensnared. We
will see.

Reconciled to tomorrow, we rejoice in the now. Be
one to ferment the leaves from the trees, and
much vapour will erupt. Do not descry the orchard

left to its own devices. There is more time here to gather the life of it. Tally on.

Blake – effervescence of life. Do you come to tell a tale, or something otherwise? Do not besmirch the trail, it comes with a herald attached. Do not dwindle the mainstay, for it carries the load. What do we say here, that has not been said?

Giving us some much-needed headrest. There are festivities to be had, and ilk to said of. Be a trojan in a trojan's guise, and there will be nothing left to guide you. Do not be estranged, things will pass with a determinant flurry.

Blake – forever, this tune is it. Have a salience near the water's edge, there will be time to marry a bulge. There is something here to be given, but not thrown. What is this here? A piece of us has come loose, and fallen out of the carriage – yes.

Being one to erupt upon the stage. We see ourselves with much mirth. Much aplomb, much intrepid heat. And here we pass judgement on life, and know it to be a thing of much guile, and fortitude. We will say this much only.

Blake – Forging ahead, never once feeling insipid, always intent on the rest. Always believing things will come. A sense that flourishes even now. A curse that is not of our making, so we must renege it, if we can. Furthermore, much is said!

Fancy the aforementioned tree – we could only guess what would happen! There are things to do, and things to do! What have the ages to say about this? Let us go to the hither, and find a ruling there. Much is said indeed! Nothing to rest on now!

Blake – foraging around the base of it, we come to this. And this is where we find ourselves – foraging. And then, like a moon full of light, we see the way forward, forward in night. There comes a tension as clear as day. Clear as the way.

Spice and vigour – rooms that do not bind. There is like a receptacle, that sees through time. Never wondering, always coming to. The round thing, all things. And then, the space to continue. The space to see through, and beyond.

Blake – a sense that can turn the tide. A believing that wins people over. And here, where swords do not rise, where monsoons do not threaten, where squalls do not arrive, there is one thing we know, we are safe for the time being.

Scavenging through the mist, to that place in the wilderness, that has as its bounds each moistened step over mud and clay, for every day, for each sodden moment. We do not carry sticks and woods to make a fire. That is for the birds.

Blake – following suit, there arrives a group of people who have never left nor have never come. The slightest intransigence is felt by all. What have we come to, I hear you ask? There is more than troubadours will amend to.

Much loved, and must hated. The turning of the screw only dissipates the morning drizzle. Come now, have a sense of fun. Or else this life swallows you up, and never let's go. The tiring of legends is not enough to stop the troupe.

Blake – gathering in what we must, the trees shed their bark in time for the massaging of feelings that have not a simplicity amongst them. Here, we see something we have always felt, but simply have forgotten. Bravado!

Fashioned after something in spring. Fashioned after the whereabouts of the storm. It is here, where we seek, where we find, where the mainstay lurks. It is here where the finding of sharks in seas of white, seas of grey. What more is there?

Blake – cannons that do not go off. People that search that little bit further. What is left to us, is not here, nor there, nor up in the air. Going closer to the rock, seeing it fade, then sparkle (as it should). There will be more to come.

Gushing, and wishing, and sending all to the top of it. There is nothing more to say here. Nothing more to do. And here, where the rain is steady, but not lingering, we see what we have come for. What is this weather for? We will find out.

Blake – do you see the way, the way through? Is this what you call it, when you arrive? Is this what the dilettante has for us – moisture upon moisture, and through the daze of life. There comes a mixture of the ready and the high born. Come.

Aridity, and the distance to foreclose. We see ourselves in forty minutes time, and know that example will suffice. Running to believe, we catch more than a glimpse. What is this we see – once and for all. All for once. Speciality.

Blake - decidedly in fashion, like it if you will. A sense that we have made time, and made it our own. Do not disparage, things are at their right side. Nice and difficult, certainly explains the process. But what of this! Easy as a flute.

William Blake

A dreaming that has led us here. A dreaming that does not know when to stop. Through fire, and famine and all amount of hardship we have come for the battle cry to be sounded. And here love and loss and the night time of deliverance. Come.

Blake – is this the thing that doesn't sleep? Is this the thing that heralds time? Do we see ourselves again, in replete regalia? Is this what it takes, to be in command of the language? Come now, force the way through, we are there.

Harking back to times past, and forward to times future. There is like a temporal blast that has for us new nouns, new pronouns, to reckon by, and reckon with. Just disposing on the while, there is now a sense that comes in sheets. What is that?

Blake – something surging, and in charge. Something not missing, but found. Indeed, profound. And then, despite the easel and the frame, there rings a clumsy bell. In this bell is the sound of spring. In this bell is everything.

Come and take us, this bell says. Come and take us! But to where, I hear you say? But to where? To where the fox does not hunt. To where the salmon swim upstream. To where ice sits on lonely windows. And there, there we have it.

Blake – do you sit here as well? Do you tell yourself that things are made for play. Is this what we have need of – this imagining. And here, there is a recall of the past, that has as its well, a piece of the finite of life.

Solid, and in shape – (still), there is a new connection to be heard. One that has the sound of cacophony still ringing in our ears. And this place, has nothing but the motion of irreducible dilemma as its heart and species.

Blake – Silence, and the movement of the sea. Catching hold of something important. A distant memory, one that holds the key. There are many ways to be bound, but this by far the most intriguing. Be the life, it will suit.

Farming to new levels, we have the time of our lives. And here, where the lives of us all are deeply carolled, we find time in-between things to settle and enjoy. What is more, we find the well full of water, and ready to drink.

Blake – what do you see, O father of the sea? What do you feel? In-clement rising. There is something more to say here, and we will say it. What is this thing you are? - If I can phrase it like that. What is this thing that you are? Time will tell.

William Blake

Wholesome, and resting – having time. Resting and not languishing, being the time it takes. Being the sky to the stars. Being what is left, and all that is. Being shadows on the path. We have nothing else to give. But we carry on, regardless.

Blake – is this how long it takes? Is this where we are led? Is this the way forward? Is this the way back? We are not tied here, like some things. We are only here under compunction. And then, like water running down our backs, away! and through!

What do we say that you know about the world? Are you a scientist? – no you are an artist! Yes, oh my, and here, with double leaves on, double what bothers us so. And then, I say to you, there is nothing left of the hills – but what of it?

Blake - much has come of us, much that interests those that count. We must pick up the pieces and carry on. Carry on to the turbulence that is the world. Do not stop, for any man nor woman, nor tree fallen in the wind.

There is time enough to be the person we want to be. And here where the snares of life do little to harm, there is a tumbling down hills of grass, just for the fun of it. And when we are finished, we run to the tope once more, and roll down again.

Blake – nestled in deep, we come for life. And in this movement, that harks the herald's call, there lies life, and the fledging sorrow. For this we sew deep, and for this we sew sure, and for this we simply do more than before.

A feeling we once had, that is now in the distance – but what we have left is not for the choosing. Be a soothing in one time or another, and what we feel will solve all. Do not be kind, but let go of all. Do not be the willing in the strident pose.

Blake – is this the real thing, as it turns for home? Is this what we have never thought? Is this what the chain has bound to the rock? Is this what the hearty has for motion. Do not be the claim on the stairs of life. There is no price to pay.

Forever sure, forever new, forever wishing for the vanquished. Coming through the gate at speed. Coming through air in time to the never may care. And then, despite everything, we feel our way home, and into our ramshackle bed.

Blake – is this the way we have come? Through the meadow, over rock and dale, intwined with the thistle, and then through! There is a marsh in this very direction, one that carries all we need – all we must do is find it, and lo, we are there.

William Blake

The swansong of every life – it is here, and true, and for the most part everything. Everything comes here, eventually. But what we hadn't noticed, was that the tiring of life is not the end, but rather the beginning, and it is here we search – again!

Blake - a forest full of trees. Listening for the rocks to come. Listening for the rain to fall, and the stars to shine. There is now something that has as its envelope the transfiguring of the small. Do not come to pass. Yes.

Amelioration and the way. We come here to speak our heart. And here, where we are left to what is left, we signal a further foray into the neverness. It is like the feather at dawn – it is like all that is. It is like the weather on a pane of glass. This much is true.

Blake – how high do we go? How much do we have left? What is more, there are simplicities that bind, and bindings that show the way. Come and see the tenacity of things. Right on the que. I have never seen this!

I have been high, and low, and in-between. When low, teeth work was required. When high, I could see the blue sky. When in-between, as is. There was never anything more than this, this feeling I now have.

Blake – being involved with the breeze, there is no greater thing. Being transcendent is something to be awed, Blake and then, when we expect nothing less a new meeting, one greater than the last. I will wear my pithy helmet.

Seeming not to care – the way around inches past. And here, where the light casts its pall down the street, a new sense of pride, one we cannot do without. And here where things cascade in beauty, an infinite abundance of light. Crucial.

Blake – coming closer, all the more feeling. Coming closer, all the more desire. Coming closer, wandering steps. We will clinch our direction from the map, and see how much is in readiness. This much is sure – yes, hurray.

Foraging in winter gloom, we know not what to expect. But here, where the moisture in the air rises, there is warmth of the way. And with this comes joyous abandon! And here we come to celebrate, we know the times are with us. Yes.

Blake – coming in too close, says the driver – a never ending fire slide. There must be air between these receptacles, we have to say. And then, without thought, nor care, there is much to do – we will do it, to our hearts content.

William Blake

Gaining in polish, the sounds of the after-year bemuse us no end. We have here what cannot be seen, nor rivalled, nor talked about quietly. There is nothing left of this to excite. But wait, here it is! I think, indeed that was excitement!

Blake – are you to express yourself in your dotage? Of course, this much is true. And then, without the slightest compunction, you rise to the challenge. There is now merely the dusk to welcome us home – and we will take it.

Finding our feet, our sea legs don't embark on their way. I am here to say, some things last, and then further from that, we must say, the glove that binds, binds hearts. And this will do us until now. On the foreshore.

Blake – allowing for the sense to come up again, we sit, and twiddle our thumbs for a bit. But there it is, a most amazing adventure has been born. And here, with great camaraderie, we commence on our way, not even looking back.

Do not fight the light. Do not share the fair. The time it takes to harness a horse in this light is not what we expected. But still, it was fun – and the fun continues, at the fair. But still nothing beckons quite like this. We will have fun.

Blake – do you amaze us again? Is that important for you! Your corpus does not linger, but comes in full mast, round the cape, with sails, no greater thing. We are here with you, on your journey through the sky. Have no fear, this is for you.

Tempestuous, and brittle. We rain down in shards upon the hill. But what is left is not enough to trickle the future, and have it water down. Be the thing that binds, and what will be left will have the semblance of everything.

Blake – what motion do you have? What stake do you claim? There is never ointment when needed. Be a sense that things will come. The future, and belief, where these two things collide. Never mind the necessities, some will be there.

Verily, and with punch. Without the compunction to distance from, there is now something to agree with. The most impassioned speech we have yet to hear. Let it be said, there is none better. Blistering, and in tune with life.

Blake – are you listening? Did you hear the news? Did something startle you like never before? – is this where we cradle the sun, on the back of lover's quarrels? Did the sky erupt like a night without quiet? We are here for the time of it.

William Blake

Much like the centre of things, the harbour rings true. Do not feel your way upwards, there is cause for celebration. We are left with something special. And here where the climate is temperate, and the stars align (sometimes), pictures and song.

Blake – are you one to smother life, or one to exude it from every part of your body? There lingers something more than this. Life, you govern, but what of the tide? What of plating of poplars in time to us all? Diminishing, and increasing. Set for fate.

A sand in the meadow, something that rings like iron. We have the strength of ten oxen, and the force of a nightly scribe. Being like the road, we come to the fork, and know which way to go. Much debate follows, and then respite.

Blake – singing to the world, and hearing nothing back. Bellowing at the might of things, and hearing the delectable cry. And then, without reproach, a tenderness that at times overwhelms. Be in touch, there will be a fever pitch to attend to.

Mysterious and mystical – verging on the unhinge-able – verging on the sense it takes to bowl a will. Mischief made, and then succumbed. Due to the filament in the way, there is nothing left to abandon. So, sticks are here, let us come.

Blake – Where were you last spring? – there was something I wished to say to you. It matters not, not now – before I sign off on this, there is something I wish to say to you, something else – watch the dark, it is here we lie fallow.

Grainey, and with a slight touch of measurement. This is what it takes. This is what it takes. Be the tempest, and life will gain its accompaniment. Do not swallow the water, only have it at a distance, if that makes sense. Crowd in, and feel the wave.

Blake – are you the vociferous one? Is this what stands in the way of nothing, nothing disposed of? Listen carefully, this might be the one way that is forlorn, but acceptable. Do not denigrate the storm, it comes from hiding strictly for you.

Amazing, and completely fine. There is now, dispensed a whole in the fabric of things, right down to the very bottom. Have not the fear of it, there is wellness in these bones. For, without the nit-picking of life, there is nothing left.

Blake – measuring things like someone possessed of the function. Being astute, like a familiar student. There is now all the more reason to still our weary bones, and have heart - we will return. That is in us after all.

 Aghast, and with feeling. Never likened, to the end of it, through the sides of it. Come now, be in the wrestle with the world. Be now, and the past will thank you. Reservoirs of distaste, and tinder shells for the runners.

Blake – sensing the avarice, we curtail things that have no heart. Belated and storied through, there is a makeshift fence we have placated. Do not impede the ranges of things, they are fragile. And here, there is taste, and finery.

Pair shaped, and rattled. Where do we go from here? Quite nicely, straight ahead, and down, through the heathers, and up through the pines. Verily, verily, what can be said, must be said. What we motioned to when we last headed over.

Blake – a willowing in the wind, that never once renounces view. Compassion in the side-roads that whispers new names. A feeling that is here to stay. Crossed fingers, and merry larks. We have never known a time like this. Come now, speak.

Avocations, and the need to be. There is taste here, taste from the front. Do not belittle the sense of it, it will calm on its own. Feeling like slumber that has no room. We will not let go, for any price, nor any domain. Stick to it.

Blake – a roundabout way of doing things, that has heart as it has a store. And in this place, a further writing, one that has no distance, nor repose. And then, like so much that has gone before, a tension that lies to the west, and seeks the east.

Confounding, and new found love. A sense we have that the making of the sun is enough to bleed us dry. Forgive the road, here is enough to give. A well-wishing, one that gives its heart to journey. Do not relinquish the night – it is for us.

Blake – confusion reigns! Only here, does the rain reign. Be the upholding, and chance will be with you. Be the sign to pass, and the earth will move in your favour. There is here something we haven't missed. Be a cloud, and then love.

Most insightful. Most roundabout. Most deliverable. Most pronounced. Most delightful – and here where the sun does not shine, warmth is from the fire. Warmth is of the earth, and the trees, and old and the young. What is there left – nothing.

William Blake

Blake – menacing, and marauding, baring teeth, and all. Baring the semblance of happiness – does that count here? No body knows. But that is okay. We will find a way, that has no fear to tread, and no vista to be seen.

Amidst it all, there can only be nothing left. But that is okay, nothing is all we need. Placatory, and to the point. Placatory and in need of venom. Placatory, in the wind. What have we more, but the silence as it moves

Blake – what is left of us? What is left of our body, to be retained, and through, and around? What have we succumbed to? Ah, nothing. Sweet nothing. There are linkages in the water ways that have no commonalities. Speak on!

Feeling like the chain will not be enough! Feeling like things are in their proper place. Do not move a muscle. There are times to tread carefully, and times not. And here, where the windblows, and the windows shake. Here we see ourselves again.

Blake – are you smothered in oil, at the first guess? What have you seen, a ghost? Is this what tortured you so – points of domesticity? Do not lag feelings are remiss. And when they come, they come in a flood. This much is made true

Falling, falling for the horizon – the great divider. And here where we sail for our lives, a new breeze will have us, and have us still. A neckline, and a figure rounded to repute. Be the chance we have to settle unto new shores.

Blake – are you the settling, settling of modes of reminiscences? If so, do you see yourself in bronze, in gold, in iron. The noise the centre makes at times like this is enough to seize upon. Do not perplex! The rough and the meaningful will obey.

The sempiternal and the glowing. Have for ourselves the pitch and the feather - along with the farming of the desolate regions, there is a time for this, it remains true. There are sisters of this world that catch on the penumbra of the sun.

Blake – where were you, when the patterns on the walls faded? Where were you, when the nape of our necks shuddered at the possibilities? And here, and there, there is a time to be ensnared, but also a time to escape.

A further belief that does not fade, is here amongst the heathers. But what we saddle up to, is not a trusty stead, but rather our shadow, a thing that bears no fruit, but can protect us it times of trouble. Do not feel for us, we are simply excited.

William Blake

Blake – a hand full of dust, that does not know its boundary, nor its opposition. There comes a time for sense amongst the nonsense. A time for passion in amongst the sword. There is a place for all things, in equal measure. Never give in.

A fortuitous thing, this life. Once it thrives, and twice it dives. And here, the majesty of life only graduates in a chosen fold. But what of this, in all its grace – a letter from a friend in times of difficulty and hardship. We write back, in swiftness.

Blake – a fusion of fabrics, of watercolours on the base of it, of this you have much knowledge, and of gold-leafing! That can never be determined in its sage like capacities. When the inanimate becomes alive. When things thrive despite!

Advantageous, and renewed. Forever sanctified, and with heart. Never listened to, but still in shape. A sort of catching onto the sides of things, a sort of dying that is living. A sort of grandeur that is lived here, lived for the sake of nothing more.

Blake – assignations, and conditions of delivery. Having a time of it, and not knowing why. Having more than what is left. Have a sense we can make it. Due diligence, one that holds on tight. One that vipers straight to the heart.

Affirmations, and what is left. A consignment of the best, from a well-spring to the left. And here, where most of us curtail, the grimacing is for the hedgerow, and the seeming intransigence of it all remains the same. Further points of stature.

Blake – Blake, do you stand out above so much, above the hills even, above the country, above the sky, above the stars – is there a Blake constellation? I bet there is. And now, with grandiloquent aplomb, something we will do to calm!

Giving adhesion to the life. Giving what is near, and can never be far. Giving what is linking by inclusion onto the very fibres of life, we send ourselves far and through and around. Never come for real, only in turns of round appeal.

Blake – a high set insistence, one that has as its daily movement a daily walk, around and through, and beyond – but mainly through. And here, where the silence rings truest, we come to find love, if it can be found – do you agree?

Assiduous and through and through. Being nearer to the edge of things, than further. Being in a state

William Blake

of calm, that follows all things. Having more than is windswept. We have never seen the mystical here, although we have tried.

Blake – further news from afar – who has written you, Blake? Who has written a missive? Who, Blake! It is sometime since we have seen that style, so particular, so precise. I would see things differently now – and then, again!

Come and be a merchant of the way through. The door is small, but the land beyond utters much that can be said. Opportunity in the willows, and all that comes. We have not seen the enchantress for some time.

Blake – pursuing all of the entrenched, bliss is now in front of us. And behind us, only fair troupes. And then a bevy of deliverables comes to obviate nature. Have as a musket trick, all the movement of Job. Come to the fair ground, it suffices!

A litter of things to come. A litter of the new ways to be. A litter of found and scored. There is half than can be tarnished, there is less than can be held. And then, a new visage, one that persists through, and into. Be a wilderness, it will help.

Blake - fashioning a new design, one for the plates
for your books! Maybe a repartee design, we will
call it! No, Blake is not pleased -fair enough, why
change the immaculate. Why go and change what
is sturdy, and studied!

Vestiges of life, there are two - alive and together.
But what of the nearest folk, some people who
hold the carriage through the night, and those who
never relinquish hope? Come and be the tendrils
to the morn. There is something here to dance to!

Blake - administering the medicine that cures all.
This is what you do Blake. But what is left cannot
be found. What can only be found are the tendrils
of love and fate. Never will we see them together.
This time is ours. This time is ours.

Foraging through the sea, for treading and for
diving, the mystery of the sea. Many have come to
partake of this mystery, but none have given
guidance to see it emerge. What have we found?
Nothing that heals as it gives. The sea.

Blake – a wishing, and a movement to the left.
Hope you can swim. Hope you can dive deep to
collect sand from the bottom. There is here, a sort
of mainstay, breathing in, diving, surface,
breathing out. Hope you can swim.

There is here a chance at the newness of the spring. Water for everybody! Come and see what we can see. And now, back to the main road. And here, where the people line up to see your work Blake, we are back to your time!

Blake – every given grain of sand has its world as every heaven has its wildflower. This much has as its range the peaking of the good. But what we don't see is how far down these things go. All the way down, or half. Still good for all you hear.

Gaining in momentum, the harbouring of hope lets us see what we want to see, feel what we want to feel, travel where we want to go. There is a belief that things will not be outweighed, and now, never bent in wrong directions.

Blake – are you interested in your own foibles as well others? This is something we know as a trace, that comes in land sized portions, and gives us more time than ever to see the invective as it runs up hills, and down again. Never still.

Severing ties with the night. But how can we? It is so verdant, and together with all we call ourselves. Dreaming of the past – this much is true. But what of the night? Where rabbits lie in wait, and we see ourselves not without time.

Blake – an ascension to believe in. What is that
my friend? You believe already. I have no doubt.
Singing in the sycamore tree. That is what bends,
and what sees us through, and what has the
minus to the plus sign

Symbiosis, and living on top of it all. We cannot
recall a time more dreamed of than this. Much as
we liked to talk about it. Much as we liked to be
the one that chills the stars, much as the
confederacy lingers together. Be still, my heart.

Blake – holding on, through this time and the next,
there is a demand on all of us, but we never
acquiesce. The times say please, but we say no.
And there begins another adventure, one of the
soul, and wit, and charm.

Forging ahead, there is steam at our lodge. Steam
at the very time and place we hold dear. Do not
forget this place, we still live in awe of it, until age
weakens us, but lets us live, so we still think, and
remember. The tautness of time.

Blake – are you the one to see things up the right
way? Is this your diminishing retreat? Can we live,
now why die? Is this the way we speak when there
is nothing left to argue about? Let me know what
you are thinking!

William Blake

Having the fold on the table, never one to subside – clawing at the wind to get some attention. We will win this fight, and the fights of those that follow after us. There is nothing after this, except for this – we question everything, and win!

Blake – tethering along without mischief. Forever foreboding, and always disowning. A symptom of the fire, at a loss to really see. There can only be one thing left to do, and that is run, as straight as you can, for as long as you can.

A mention made of the storm, one that rings true. One that has as its base the utmost clarity. Come now for the wind of it. There is a winter to be had, and we will have it. And then, more of the same – but yes, the storm – the storm.

Blake – conscious of the need we all have, conscious of the sand we all have. Conscious of the sense of it. Conscious of the degrees of separation. The desire, the hours, the winnowing, the regret. May we come in times of glory.

A forest of trees in the wind. What we thought was the end is only the beginning. What we had always admired, until nothing else mattered. What we now love more than ever, until the legacy remains. Catch this, trouble is gone.

Blake – a suite of the accomplished – a victory of sorts – a new time, and a new vantage. There is something that allocates the suffering in proportion to lived lives. What we get is our allotment, to carry us forward. What say you?

Forgiving, not holding on, not seeing twice, not veering into, not overloading. With these things in place, we will go far. But without them, what can never be in tune. Favour and the slow silence. Come with it – we will try!

Blake - erudite and accomplished, four score and ten. All the more beholden, the closer she comes. What is left of the dance, when the dance is done? Come for tactics, when tactics are all that are left. There comes something more.

Home spun, and endearing, following on from things to come – what was once, and now and then, utmost to the time of it. Sequined and elongated, never quite there, but always there. Can there be more than this? Let us see.

Blake - Hoping against hope, there comes a fastidiousness to counter all claims. But here Blake, there is enough of the lid, and more of the sense of it – something to weave in and out of. Something we can still at a touch. Yes we can.

Higher and higher, ever higher. And here, where the land rears from slumber, and the moon is full, something comes to linger nightly by these things we have never known. Catching the fullness of the reflection, we leap up, and say yes to the night!

Blake – gaining traction, there are things that never sleep. And here where the motion of the planets is spherical once again, we move through sweetness, like an attraction that doesn't linger. Can we ever find the way? We will see.

Sparkling, and intrigued. What is here is never there. What is there is never here. What we have is never a modicum, but what is left is other than us. Feigning blindness, we sense the way forward. Never a chance to weave backward.

Blake – a sense we have that the right way is with us. A sense we have that things can no longer be treacherous. The middle of this thing. The middle of this thing. Rise up and see ourselves through. Rise up, and move the party onwards.

Gregarious and followed around. Gregarious and sorted out. There is an ounce of life left here. An ounce of life left. We will eat some more, and see how we go. What is left now? We will wonder until tomorrow. And then, yes then.

Blake – an afternoon in the sunshine, is this what says to you, yes I am here! Some hold the winter is best, localised heat in the cold. There is now a question for you, do you stay, or do you leave? We will mark time – you will stay!

Dragging out the missives from your past, Blake, what do you find? All sorts of emotions and situations, and excitements, and decisions! All of this, through and through. Some distances, as much as can be explained. All sorted!

Blake - a ride here, a ride there, never once envisioned, not for an ounce of tea. There comes a time, for the sake of it, that never once tarried to consider. It is here, that we come to ice the garden pagoda. We are there!

Never again will we cross these boundaries. Never again, in this book, will be go beyond time and place. And here, there is a wind, that rains as it moves, and comes down as it fathoms. See the one that is missing, that is the one we need.

Blake – never before seen, or done, like something from the aether. We mill about it, as if time had stood still, and then, like a place in the shade, we come closer than we ever have. But what have seen, but everything that is unseen. We are there.

William Blake

Narrow-gate onto the street. Narrow-gate onto the road. Narrow-gate to see us faring. What does it see? All a-gate. There is time to be sad, and time to be glad. And here, where the life of it is like a windmill, we see what is coming, from afar.

Blake – never yet foretold, always loving through, and there is space, space to reckon with the spirits – the same as guided your hand, Blake. Come now, we have sent for the for the best spring water – will you partake?

Treasuring the time we have left. Being allied to the twilight. Things that turn grey, and then white. A nauseating effort, one that always lives. Have you seen all this today, it defies description. And here, on the fence, a way to be – not for us!

Blake – a unique turn of phrase, what was it – it was just out of earshot for us. And now, a semblance of the night, one that grows larger in the years to come. A semblance of the night – we will honour it out of respect to its breadth.

Being in touch with so much. Having a heart that beats. A silence at the end of things. More than it's worth. A spectacle to see. All the basics. Something we really ought to see. There is now time enough, we will come for the light.

Blake – a solemn movement, one form here to there. A solemn cry, over and above. What we thought was something is nothing. What we thought was nothing is nothing. Do not move here, the tension is all. We will find a way.

Come for the play on rules. Come for the mystery of acceptances. Be the bird of prey, and see yourself fly! There is a change in the air. No longer brisk, but biting. Hold yourself to account. Be the sting in the tail – nothing dares.

Blake – a holding on to things that never lets go. A feeling we once knew. Poems that stream through the air. A longitude to match the latitude. Given a price, and being calm. There was once service in these words.

Being a little cautious, and then being rattled, but coming through. The best portion of a fine meal. The listening that is done to guide. And then, like an explosion in the night. All the more reason to see ourself, and then some.

Blake – foreshadowed, but not overlooked. Given time, but not allowed to be. Things that are enjoyed, but not to the degree of fate. Give us what we need, says an up-standing citizen, and in this a whole new dimension of things. Come, be loved.

What the sea says. What the sea says goes. What the sea says goes twice. What the sea doesn't say, more importantly. What we have said instead. There is now an ambition to be the world, as it rocks to and fro. We have yet to sink, this much is true.

Blake – utmost attention, and the figuring of speech. There is more to say here, so let us say it! There can only be one thing, in this life, and that is heart. Everything else pales. And here where the darkness doesn't rally, new found hope.

What have we said, but everything. There is a noise in the casket, it is not us. There is a noise, it is not us. But what we have, is something special, away from such matters. There is a time for play, more so now, than before.

Blake – having what the kitchen believes. Being now in time to things strictly. There is a valuable embrace near where we sit. It is all that we have, and all that we will be. What is left of us, is something that we can almost comprehend.

What matters now, now that we know of the way through? Now that we have come full circle, and lives are no longer embittered? This is what we say to the night, as we walk that long walk we always do. Never flinch, always rally!

Blake - I have often heard it said, that life pertains to the unwary, for it is they that can swim the estuary of reality with much more vigour. What have you to say about that? And it is in this capacity that gives them an almost drastic power over things.

And then, like a region of wear, that casts no shadows, we are here to fully button things as they are. And then, without the tomb stone to keep us, we look forward to what is done, and what will be done. And this brings a whole new ring to things.

Blake – uneasy at the helm, we sit back, and watch things unfold. There is now something we can tell of life and love and loyalty and devotion, and that is all four are a good place to start, but then we must extend ourselves through and over.

Conditions are good for the course, and here we state what we need, and follow in search of a retraction or two. The only way to see the way through, is to hammer home the home grown truths. And then despite everything, a simplicity to be had.

William Blake

Blake – cautioned, and withheld, new forms of moisture, new forms of happiness, despite the ringing in the ears, and then a sort of hanging on, that lasts and lasts and lasts, and then piece by tiny piece, away, and away again. Yes, today.

Aforementioned time. Aforementioned sea. Aforementioned heart. What have we done with all that is. What has come in the fullness of the arc. Temperance and the lifting of things higher. We are not afraid to laugh, so we will.

Blake – whispering things I have never heard before. Whispering deeply, and without breath. There comes a wizard to calm both, and the silence he beckons knows only the tenacity of a fob watch. Coming to the core of it, we stand.

There is like a station at heart, one that orders out of bounds, and then relinquishes the same, in spits and spurts. Come now, do not be in the in-between here, there is more to be sure of than a wolf cavalcade. We will be here.

Blake – The reticent and the relieved. Somehow without the need to be. There is fibre in these parts – the fibre of the world. Never wanting more – simply in love with it. A sense we have not to surrender. A sense we have to keep going.

All the more reason not to do something. All the more reason to let go. All the more reason, to see ourselves famished for the journey. And then, like a spark in mid-air, something falls in front of us, and has as its stapple all the wheat we need.

Blake – mystery, and artifice, being there where nothing really should. And then without commitment, an arrival that beckons, and says, yes, I am here. There is a tenacity here that runs deep, deeper than anything before.

Full and at speed, the burrow we whisper to has an undulating frame, better for the carrying of food, and the undulations of a populace. Come and stand with us, dear man, there is more to do than ever. More to do now that every before.

Blake - inching forward, we see ourselves divide a path, inculcated, and shining through, we laugh with no regret. And here, there is a wonder that doesn't pass. A wonder that looks through the grave, and says yes, we are there. Well done.

Faust like, and Mephistopheles round given, there are places that do not shed their water like a kindred spirit, with sequences at large, and fallings emptied, and then a whole sequence of the replete, and then we come once more, yes.

William Blake

Blake – coming first, and then last, and then first again! Gregarious and not shaken. Gregarious and not seen, there is a love that tends to all flocks. There is a heart that has as its tender all the will of the world. But what is next?

Allegro, and in time to life. Missing a beat, but not saying so. But then a hardy laugh, that sends us to our knees. What is this? This playing at nappers and followers? All the more willing to fight for the division we are all in.

Blake – Moncrief, and alabaster, sitting in the rain. There is a tangent we must win at. There is a window we must see through, there are things we must do, and things that must remain undone! Through to the end. No to offend.

Mystery and sacrifice. We read through what we think is the news, but sparkles as something else. Do not hold on to what is said here, only regurgitate what you need. And then, with superlatives at hand, we fence with the postmaster to the now.

Blake – solving all problems, the withholding of talk perplexes as it moves. And then height to the masses, height to the thousands! Those who want it can have it! There will be many takers. Many recalcitrant takers. We are in sync.

All the more to commandeer the ship and reign pebbles on the water below. We are here for the vexatious, and not for our sort. Do not tarry long, the most we can say is that the hard and the solo is hardly of a vest on material. Be brave, we will come.

Blake – moisture in the run of it. Moisture in the brief of it. A stay in proceedings, that farrows a noise made for climbing. And then the hard way through. Never a second glance. Until that point where magnificence rears, and temples dissolve. Yes.

Most high and exalted one – come here, let us duel. Fight the fight of the hydra, and all that she stands for. Much is needed on this front – there are complexities unknown here, and there, and everywhere. But we will come for nothing else.

Blake – a sensational start, given credence by the lark, there is now no sense to be willing. And then, like a gasp of fresh air, in the side of the mouth, there resists the tapestry of light, thrown down, from on high, and given life therein. Yes.

Forging through, and in and beyond. Much wood has been burnt at this base. And without a further care, we send ourselves again into the fray, the deep fray. And in this a diamond forms beneath our feet, and in this we know strength. We must.

Blake – Come and see the way of it, there are multiple places to start. And in this way, we do start from the place given to us. Sure of our need, and our lack of greed, there rings a true sound. It rings deep into the air, and we all hear it. We must.

Grassy plateau, and fine on the hill. We have a lot to be thankful for, and a lot to hope for, so let's hope, and let us be thankful, and then let us cry into the mug of eventualities. There are things we cannot see, and things we must see.

Blake – it is as if you were never here. We sensed that from the very start. But what have we to know, except all that rings with truth, and says sorry to the dawn. There is a splendour here, one that goes on to see things clearly.

Gaining ground, who are we to say towards what. Let us have the fight back in us, the fight against the times. And then, with a certain slowness, we get ready ourselves, and believe that the crystal chamber knows its own way.

Blake – a harbouring, and a mist, and a fog, and all that will be, and all that will be chasten, and linked to the earth, for here it comes, again, and through and yes, then silence. Encompassing through, and around – don't be slow, nor quick.

Share on displays of pomp and ceremony. There is nothing like any of it to really find ourselves into. The cost is high, but so is the pleasure – what is more is that finding the right place can be a godsend. Watch for the snow fall, it comes to please.

Blake – is that you? All the way down there, is that really you? We have more questions for you! And here they lay, all nice and clean. What is your favourite book – the Marriage of Heaven and Hell. Your favourite Epic poem – Milton!

Alright and down with it. Alright, and through with it. We will not judge any of it, for what is in store for the pioneers on the frontier, for anytime, nor any place. Come for the mystery, and not the rite - spring or otherwise.

Blake – singing down the road, there is nowhere left to go. Having the spirit to rise again, where rising is a formidable thing. I will rise like no other, no other than truly is. There can only be one stop on the vine, the vine of love.

William Blake

Arching away, and giving it all of our gusto. Seeing ourselves disappear over the horizon. Much is said, and much is duly noted. We must send ourselves quite to the edge, and then back again, through the hoops of fire. Yes, this is it.

Blake – entangled, and wolf thrown. Never really witnessed. A sort of farming that doesn't require. What we saw was a fence in the distance. Much loved, and involved in the motion. Triggered, and belated, but still at call. New, and invigorated.

Making our way in, but not lately – there are scars to tend to. We have nothing left to show for our troubles, but that is fine. We are there where we would like to be. We are here, where sand does not sheer – where the lot does not cry.

Blake – holding on to things, having the brass, and listening to. What is it that we have not heard? What is it that the sky has not told us? What is it that the fingers of unease have now rendered? We are not left with much, but enough.

Burgeoning with life. Burgeoning with hope. Burgeoning with the beginning of all things. There is a test to our very souls, which we can easily pass if we let it. Never before have the sands of it been on display for so long.

Blake – offering up the dust of a city street. It is
the street we live on, so we take strength from it.
There is now the trend of ancient windows, to
once again, be open, open and free. And that is
what we find ourselves with! Aha.

Neglecting nothing but the air, which we breath
easily enough. Sojourns and summers in wait.
And there, wrestling the door to the ground, and
having our say of it. What can we do, but be the
health of it? Be a sense of belonging. Yes.

Blake – there is a strength here, one that never
languishes. But wait, a turn of speed greets us
home, and then a solemn retreat, one that has
been marked by the centuries, and now, come
and be the well-spring of fate. Joy, and bliss.

Committed, and yet not divided. A passion that
rises in the way things are. A fashion that can no
longer be appraised, except here. There is much
more to do, and much to undo. Have we our riding
gloves, they will help no end.

Blake – a tethering, and a shawl. No two ways
about it. And here, despite everything in turn, a
note of optimism, one that belongs to the west
wind, and breaths harder under cover, in wisps of
whirly breeze.

A fading light – one that stays the course. One which has as its recompense the night sky. One which harbours light as a denizen does in amongst it. Never been seen. Never more than a question. Never lasting, always going.

Blake – somethings are raucous, and somethings are not. Some things find the where-a-bouts, but there are those who can't see. Have the moisture in it rise, and see what happens. Have that which can't be seen, come to you.

Alignments of tests that must concur. A shortage of land that harbours no grief. There are things that come straight on. There are nuisances that find a place. And here, what is more, there comes a treaty, not to disparage. Ever.

Blake - a place you like the best. Travel there, and see what happens, see what the load can bring. See what the load can do. See what is ever reluctant in the mist of it. There is a chance, while here, that there have been noticeably fewer grass towers

A sense of what is left. A sense of what life can give. A sense of the middle page of a book. And there it is – right through, turn around, give a slap, let the boundaries revolve – but around what? Around the few, and the parcelled.

Blake – never arising until it is late. Never in the slightest moment, one thing to cherish - could there be more to say here? Could this be the way of it – right here, right now. This much is still in the confines - more than enough, I will say.

A tired adventurer, coming in from the rain. Does this mean more dice? Or less? Probably more. But that is okay, for when we wink, we do so with all the charm of everybody that has winked before – without looking sanguine.

Blake – a nestling of things to come – a sorrow that leads many places. What is here, is the strength of years – but we don't call them that, and like you, we call them the strength of experience. There are places to go with this.

The sea, the raging sea. With a guinea, we buy the world. With a pound, we buy what's left. There is much in this world that demands attention, but afternoons are here for the taking. But what else is there? We have all we need.

Blake - forging away in summer fields, we enclose ourself tightly in what is to come. Blake, do you wear the sort of clothes you should, for your standing – I am thinking of a high shirt collar (white), with high jacket collar (black)!

William Blake

The cushion at the end of three seats – no time for comfort today, we sit on each of the three seats in turn. And have our fun at this round table of larks. And then with saleable items amused, we find something else in our future.

Blake - such a pity there is no-one to lace up these shoes. And here, where the smallest thing becomes a blemish, we will ride forth into another way of thinking, another way of being. And there, in recovery mode, something special.

The smallest thing believed in; the smallest thing retained. And now, without the newest spot of the cavalcade ever reaching, we send forth our ideas to catch the wind, and in this a mighty burden is lifted – you will see.

Blake - a mysterious phenomenon, is the past. I have lived there for five years, plumbing the life of letters in the 19th century – French and now English -A strange thing the past – but we will see ourselves anew because of it!

Apprentice to the world – feeling august, and seeing how it ends. Never once looking back, always looking forward. Having the taste for it. Never once disbelieving, forever in the mode of it - we will fight until there is nothing left!

Blake – a caustic entry on to the stage – what more is this? What more is this? We linger in the waiting room, never knowing what to do, or what to say. And then, a small piece of advice we had never thought of – and then, well yes, again!

Forests that never blow over – the trees are too thickly bunched together. But when they come close a strength kicks in, and never over they go. Moisture only makes them grow, and the animals that live in the forest depend upon them.

Blake – a sense the waves of the sea have that forward is the right motion. But what is more, is that the time that is had by all, is the same time, but travelling at different speeds. It is like lightning on the horizon, that stays in tune, for a while.

Aforementioned, the time of life stills, and does not give in of itself. It only mentions kindly the umbrage that is felt by an age. And here, there is a message to be read – but read only once. The taciturn commotion always wins in the end.

Blake, is this you, oh one of hearts. I am one of spades. But one of hearts is fun, forgetting the end of things. But you have the memories. But this is not a course of action – oh yes it is – and so on. Live the course, lie beneath it.

William Blake

What is there left, but the enjoyment of the mode? I have sensed more than what is wanting, more than what is chaste, more than the whole region bounced from here to there. There is a semblance of the night. We will hide from it.

Blake – does the sand run between your toes? Do things of marked spontaneity listen to what is being said? Have you marched in solemn acceptance of the world, only to reject it once again? Oils by brevity, and sense still to come.

A quintessential piece of the puzzle, known only to a few. But these few know more than the casket does. And on launching day, the sun reflects off the water with a delightful shimmy. And before we know it, yards to fill. There will be time.

Blake – fortunate that the lateness of the dark will harry along as usual. And then, like a spark in the expanse, fortune ravishes the sky in amongst the tethers of life. There is nothing here worth fighting for, but we will see the consequences.

There was once a place, a place of rest. And here, where the gumption was not for omitting, but rather of never conceding, there was not a motion like this. We toil, but not for the sum of it – but for the trail of, and in this way we tread – upstaging.

Blake – holding on to things that little bit tighter –
then we let go a little bit, and urge ourselves on
again. What is this we see? What is this we know?
What is this we believe? And then, a mischief from
the trees. We will cast again.

Settling in for a ride! Settling in for what is to
come! Settling in for the adventure of it all! Come
now, incisions don't bring speed. But what does?
What you hate the most – glorified daggers.
Daggers of the heart.

Blake - a chalk and dustbin kind of experience,
one that has as its escape all the world combined.
There is never enough to see through to the end.
Come and be my side cringe in the magic of it. We
will never see straight, but only off to the left.

A much heralded heart land – one that never
ceases. One that stops for nothing, and no one
and nobody. This land, is all that some people
speak of, but it goes through toiling away, it
provides a base for farming, and recreation, and to
be lived on!

Blake – is this your land Blake – Jerusalem. I bet
you thought it would be Felpham! And in this way
we rage around the mists of the sea, and the
dryness of the kind-hearted. Never one to miss a
beat, considerable treats are here to stay.

William Blake

What is the tempest now for you? For me, it is tremendous doubt, and suffering thrown into one, but there can only be this, so we just let it pass of its own accord, and there we go. The monument to suffering, 10-fold!

Blake – do you see what I see – do you have that capacity, very good. Is this what I look like? We revel in something here. This is what that looks like, much amusement! There is a sand to the hour glass, we must not miss it.

Much imagined, but not much saw. Much imagined, but much drawn. There are things to come, and things to be aware of. And things to see coming, and all that, and all that want. There will never be this time again. Never.

Blake – a votive mass, what do they say about Blake? There is no telling, but what we can say is the sea will be at high tide then, and then now. Then low tide, at this time, and then now. Falling on the rocks of life, we no longer bleed – Ha!

Abolished, and fought for, never sung for, but then, never listened to either, the casting around for grander things than these. We see the complexity of things, and with much courage (you Blake) set out a plan, and the assault is new.

Blake – sunny, and outdistanced. The clouds, and flocks of birds. The side of a hill, one that doesn't go anywhere. Much amused, and in being amused, being delighted. The horizon is all we need. We will ask for it, and see where it takes us.

Ascending to the stars, never a branch to early. Giving solace, and the harbours of respite. What we have come to know, through much travelling. Something that seems not quite right, but fits in anyway.

Blake – a semblance of things to come. A moisture that doesn't grow anything. And here, where sands are like the hourglass, there withholds a great monument, to the lesser-known creators. Feeling like life is a bastion, and that things after it, a rule.

Considerable weight is carried here, weight that has as its crescendo something of the night. Never once believe it to be true, unless you believe it. Never once seeing things the same way as the depths of it, until you are through.

Blake – forward, and reminiscent. Likewise, and through the sky. We have at our disposal nothing more than all. There is a time for all of this, to come down through the weather, down through the ground, then, up, and beyond!

The tears of Arabia, never smoother, nevermore luscious. We collect these tears, and know them to be great. We cannot drink them, but we can capture them, or even harvest them. This is the time for release, and a time for larking around.

Blake – do you realise what has happened? Do you see yourself abroad, and in one go, there? This much is true, that the handle piece to forever is a joint holding two hands. But that won't stop us, there is something more, twin entity!

Is there a sort of space for the margins of our lives. Blake, you were the king at margins, and here we have life, gold leafed, water coloured, prized beyond measure – these are your margins, and these are our margins of choice.

Blake – never quite knowing how to do the rest of things, we come for you, in times of tidings, and of joy, and indeed of reticence. There can be nothing more than this. We sit, and are pleased, pleased with what has gone on.

Never mind the celebration, what is tension a meaning for, for you? We travel higher, faster, taller, with softer shoes, with harder shoes, with keepsakes for luck, and then we find our rhythm, and it is gone, only to return at home.

Blake – short of the apple tree, we luxuriate for a moment. And here, where the crossing of stars only placates the few, we must have our streets as wise as yours. There is now somewhere to go, in amidst of it all.

Cycling through the corpus, we come across many fine poems, especially the epic ones, but what is more, we find life there – not the answer to life, but life exhibited with simple water colours gold leafing and outline.

Blake – much is said of these things, these things of beauty you have created, but what is not said, is how far it lifts the suffering of the world? There is time enough to see! And then, without the slightest inclination, we see Blake in his finery.

Hoping to see more, we see the gates of infinity before Blake, and his work, and all that it can be. There is a mischief of sorts here, that doesn't beckon too loudly, or too long. There is now something we hunger for, and find at our leisure.

Blake – whistling to ourselves, and never knowing when to stop. Having quite the time of it, and seeing it through. There is never one thing to say,

than what the branches say themselves.
Launching into it, and never curtailing.

A hop step and a jump. We listen carefully to the dawn, and know that the sense we have to follow the round is one of great seriousness. And then, with eyes glowing from the heat of it, there wanders in the way of it something else – we will see.

Blake – heaving open the fireplace, and knowing it to be a rich repository of life. We look back down, and see ourselves in the mirror. It is here where life truly is, nestled deep inside our bodies. We look again, and see it there. Yes, a delight.

Singing the praises of – never before have we lingered like this – lingered nightly by the grave, there is here an auction of souls, one, two, three, out. Never one to say the numerals in line with the heart. We will follow!

Blake – gorging on the wishbone, and all it accords. Never once seeing the land seek office. And then, where the wind blows in a unison that hardly knows itself, there is a temperance that steels itself for desire. It will come.

Forests, and trees, and indeed, a clearing – there is much peace here. And much to be found, much to be sought. And in the mean-time, a presence to be accorded. A presence to be needed by. There is here nothing like this!

Blake - are you the one to take us there, to where we want to go? Is this your lane, and your jettisoned party? There can be nothing more than this – riding on the vanguard of fate, pursuing all who follow. This is life!

Riding along the coast of our lives, we see so much, and so far. But what of this, what of this street. We were born here, and some have stayed. But what of the treasure of sleep – it will come, and be the one to salvage itself.

Blake – there is a missive here we never thought possible. With the right tone, and the right cadence, this letter looks likely to amaze. And then, with a soaring intact, we find words from the heart, words from our past, and words from the world!

Treasuring all that we see. There is a chance to breathe with a deeper breath. And here, despite ourselves, we come again, come for the sport of it, come for the needle in the hay stack. A belief in it all…there was once a time!

William Blake

Blake – do you stay on the ridge, waiting for Catherine – do you find her there? Do you see her now, with eyes ablaze, and ears a-tuned. Sometimes we find ourselves writing in a style that is not ours. But will it leave its mark?

Gusting with august composure. We accept our lot with not a trace of the sign-post. Repartee, and the sovereign in us all. Do we help ourselves to tea, help ourselves to star-dust, we have no other way. There will come a new time!

Blake – dancing with the Christoff's – they have come to savour the day. Savour what is left of our ease. There is never a moment like this, never a moment where we herald what is left. Come now, never enough.

The sea, it rages, it talks as if we are passed it. The sky has opened in squall, but the sea, the mighty sea! We have had enough, but we continue. There is now a clinching onto favours, and they tell our self, we can come to.

Blake – not a nice thing, this thing called life (at least sometimes). What are your wares? Where do you come from? What is the marsh that hired you? Do not render appeal, such as the night will come, and become you, in the streets of London.

And then, yes, joy and a sense of purpose. What we manage to see in the gloom, and seem to see by the candle light. A touch of the troubles – despite everything that has passed. We will find ourselves again, in play, and in wonder.

Blake – is this where you reside, along these streets, along these narrows? There is a time for catching the tide as it comes, catching our whereabouts – to and fro. But what we most need is the sense to come through finally. We will be there.

Fishing for the table to end the conversation. To be the one who drives home the home-truths, the one to seek things out afresh, and beckon to the rest of us – come, and see the final play – it is simply something we all must see!

Blake – an amnesty on what we see, and what we have in favour. Do not belittle the clothes we have on our backs, they are precious. Do not believe in what the dawn tells, it is too beautiful! And then, and now, a whisper - not of regret, but of favour.

A tenet of a larger teaching. Something there, something to think about. Something to knock you backwards, and out of shape. Dress for the climate. Dress as you please. Dress to appeal. Never just open your eyes. Simply put.

William Blake

Blake – walking forwards like never before. Striding. Coursing. Walking at rapid pace. Walking contently, being not one to laugh at the wrong moment. Come now, see the arrow of fathoming. Seek it, and know what it is for.

Walking straight through. Never a backward step of it. The tenacity delights. Come and see the way it is played here. There cannot be any other. No other, and then... And then some. Knock on wood, we are in the midst of something here.

Blake – Seraphim wax, and all that pertains to the night. What have we said, but all or nothing. What have we nestled into but life itself. Do not care to listen, there is nothing to hear. Do not cast a spell with those eyes, they will tell a tale.

Magic, as if by artifice, magic, as if by social illusion. There is a chance, through these things to know ourselves, and through that know the world. But what of it? There be a chance to see, and see clearly. Do not shirk, there will come a time.

Blake – do you encounter others like yourself? Other beings who tread the walk of the other-side? I should hope so. Such genius in isolation would not feather a stick. But what of the half of it, how does that go? Through, and beyond, that is how.

Letting go – feeling rife – never quite settling – always on the road - never mesmerising – always letting go! There is a half-tale to be wrung from the ground of it, a tale of long nights, and harboured fancy's – do not disappoint!

Blake – a rattling of kitchen utensils, that has as it bounds nothing but the bridge. And here, where we savour all meals, there is one we enjoy most of all, and that is from the deeper kitchen, one that envisages all that

Heart and soul, and what we cannot despise. Write on the ceiling, we have been here, and let us have our say into the darning room, into the night. Never procure enough to waste, no matter how difficult. Come now, enjoy.

Blake – having a rest from the build. Believing once again in things. There is a point of release, that has as its time, the rectilinear motion of the sky. There are seethings that do not hear, nor line the streets in gatherings of dust.

Fortitude, we need you. Guts, we need you. Strength of spirit, we need your call. And everything after, we need you. This is the way we proceed, through time remembered, and time forgotten, through the light weight, and the peril. This is it.

William Blake

Blake - never ending, always fashioned, distraught but living, always closing – closing in on fate. There is more to this than you think. The multiple layers of meaning teach one to be calm in the face of great odds. Mystery will rule.

Little of the doubt of it – coming and the going. Much to see beyond, and around. There is now a sense that the time will see for us, and never through us. And then, an awful state of woe, that cries out, as Blake does. Formidable and alone.

Blake – to be at the point of ruin, and to get through, that is great point of it. Holding on still, to hear the call. And then, there is this, which causes all the ruptures to disappear – a mighty thing, in this world. Do you believe?

Witnessing the great - Blake that is you! Witnessing a harvest for the gods – we will never shirk. There is much to be said about it, and much unsaid. But the wrangling of the lark, and the spirit of the unknown, are all here - let us rejoice.

Blake – soothing in the way we walk. Catching a last glance, where spring emerges. Do not gather under the rose bush, you will see. Common ground, that has as its burgeoning the flair of the mainsail.

Bumbling through, and seeing all before you. There is a mess above the trees, that can't come down. We see it afresh, and lounge about before we have a chance to breath. Sonnets, and ramshackle dreams. We will not relinquish - for anything.

Blake - an arm full of remonstration that doesn't dull the age. And here, where the missing piece of the puzzle is right before us, we come to that place that is hard to see, for all the glasses we have. Hear us now, we cannot stop!

Verily, and in need of reproof, the adventure continues. A mischief runs in different directions, and hark, we love what we see. In the night, there is a turbulence we cannot ascertain the beginnings of. But wait, there is more...

Blake – In one sense, constraint – in another, odds are at evens. Coming in the sense of it all, we find ourselves on fire, despite the languishing of an age. Never be one to laugh here, there is too much regalia to really feel, at any rate.

A new task, a feeling we thought was forbidden, is now on the way up, and here, where solace rings true, the noise of the twilight, comes to an interesting halt, there brandishes a new toying with foibles. Reach which way you must – we commence.

Blake – Have you seen the harvest? Did you bring a bag with you? Is this what the saying has in mind? Much to debate here -much to feel as steel. And then, like the ramp to the cart, new found bliss, old found heart.

Having no need – that is truth. Have all the need, again, that is truth. And then, there forces upon us a new type of sorrow – one we feel deeply, and are invigorated by. But what is this, a reversal of things? Indeed it might be!

Blake – Falling in love – falling out of love – and then with separation comes the knowledge, still in love. We come to the conclusion that passion prevails, and that what we need is nothing other than passion, to rule our lives.

Necessities that linger, and linger long. Never a turn in events quite like this. Never a sense that the time is right. But delighted at how things are turning out. Delighted yes. But what of the throng? We must not pass judgement upon them.

Blake – being in tune with so much. Having as the by-way the highway. Come now, in crimson schooling, that has no option but to tread the line.

There is a sense that options are open. There is a sense that the township will not revoke.

The insistence that the creed belongs to the chosen. The insistence that the worn-out bride will be much above the rest. And here, where the armour of aeons lies down upon us, we never belittle the cast, the cast of deliverance!

Blake – have a snake, or rather a snakeskin. Have that which you laud, but nothing else. Alright then, let's get down to it. What is it that covers you, from night to day? What is it that helps you startle once again, from night to day?

Ash covered, and crying in the night – what do we say that is, that has no boon to bless, nor likeable attention to cross out. There are plans here, to fathom all that is in the invective to do so. Much of our group is concerned, but many are unconcerned.

Blake – a mistress for each of them! A semblance of the right way, the right way to come. There revisioned, and in lessoned, like never before, like never once before. As we depart, a new message -one that tethers as it grows.

Moseying along, the tempest gains in dimensions. I see it, and see it grow, but I am not afraid.

William Blake

Things that large deserve respect – will it take me? I do not know. It could take anyone, I would imagine. But we will wait and see for us – I have a plan!

Blake – do you wander in times of wonder? This is more of a point, than a question. I see you now, as you always have been. I see you -yes indeed! But what of the life you led. Yes, I have committed parts to memory – we are sold!

Hoping for all to be done, and in that sense complete, with nothing missing. And here, where the things before us come, we sense a new calm. And it is here, that ripened fruit can be eaten, with this calm. This much is true.

Blake – do you feel yourself at loggerheads? Is this where moisture reigns? Is this where you simply are a delight? Much fragrant work to do. Much that we have no control over. But that is okay, simply followed.

Amazement, and the semblance of renown. Amazement, and what has gone before. There is enough to say yes, I am free. Yes, I am pleased. Yes there comes a breeze to tender on the way of. Caught in the middle of this and that. Yes, we will thrive.

Blake – conditions of delivery, what more is found? What more is longed for? The distance we face is not at all what we find in any other thing. We love distance as a thing procured, and not one that can give us an ounce.

Catching our breath, there is a way through, we must only wait our turn, and the things will come. Things that love, and are loved. This is what we call for in our sleep. This is what the drains of transfiguration aligned to.

Blake – seemingly lost, we come to the ends that meet. And here, where softness resides as an echo of times subsided, there is driven in the mist a hollowed sound – one that stiffens us, before it is due. Come, and have the list of it – we will!

There is a chance at things again – we know not how, or when, or where, but that feeling comes, like a subsidiary rite. Never guessing, never align, always there, never missing. I have had a guess – which way is there? And I say up!

Blake – Are you there? Do you surmise? Is there a just path to be had? We know which lines to cross, and which to leave un-crossed. Many things are possible, many things. Can we simply opt in, at any time, and simply say that is what you are doing.

William Blake

Nation-wide, we see you! Through open eyes, open hearts, and open ears. There is something here, and we will feel it - beyond each flurry of apprenticeship, beyond each sunrise, beyond each landfall. We will come, like never before.

Blake – Letting in the wind, and off the rain. Seeing what startles when we launch ourselves at it. Never once believing in otherwise. A tortured stance, that leaves us wide awake. There is something more than this, and as we say it, we peer.

A bistro effect. There stands a line in the sand – one that never moves. So are you for or against? Much improved, and much reneged upon. There is a sense that life could be a harvest. One that belittles the time, as one holds on for the next.

Blake – is this what we say, when forks are left to tune? What is more, we are here, but we can say no more. But we must away, until the stay, and until things shoulder, or renege themselves. What have we found, but all that is. Thankyou.

www.ingramcontent.com/pod-product-compliance
Lightning Source LLC
Chambersburg PA
CBHW020652220526
45464CB00001B/400